THE SPACE OF TIME

THE SPACE OF TIME

Katarina Frostenson

Translated from the Swedish by Bradley Harmon

Threadsuns Press 2024

Published by Threadsuns, High Point, NC 27268

First published in 2015 as *Sånger och formler* by Walström & Widstrand

First Edition
28 27 26 25 24 1 2 3 4 5

ISBN 978-1-7346911-6-0

Library of Congress Control Number: 2024947708

The Space of Time is set in Cambria.

WINNER OF THE 2016 NORDIC COUNCIL LITERATURE PRIZE

"*The Space of Time* is a collection to be read many times . . . for its wealth of associations, encounters between sounds and images and movements."

—AASE BERG, *Kristianstadsbladet*

"The poems are beautiful, on the verge of dazzling, and often sad. But the grief is punctured by the joy that language exists at all, that language can play."

—KHASHAYAR NADEREHVANDI, *Sveriges Radio*

"To read Frostenson's *The Space of Time* is like when autumn kills a flower, petal by petal, and to remember it as simple, beautiful."

—DAVID STENBECK, *Svenska Dagbladet*

"Frostenson is a linguist in everything she does. She seeks neither beauty or harmony, but the most precise expression of chaotic states. . . . There is no loud enthusiasm or passion in her poetry, no proclamations or big words. The reader simply has to focus and follow the cues. On the other hand, one discovers both political themes and current events in the subdued poems. *The Space of Time* is an eminent collection of poems in the proud tradition of Karin Boye, Gunnar Ekelöf and Tomas Tranströmer."

—INGUNN ØKLAND, *Aftenposten*

"As a language artist, a concerned citizen, and an everyday person, she goes where it stings. Where there is something both big and small at stake. And she does so in a way that makes you feel that she wants to express something that is vitally important."

—JES STEIN PEDERSEN, *Politiken*

"Katarina Frostenson has long had an ability to articulate feelings that have no words, to articulate the wordless. This is a quality she shares with song. . . . Frostenson has once again shown why she is considered by many to be one of the best contemporary Swedish poets."

—MATS O. SVENSSON, *Ny Tid*

"*The Space of Time* is one of her sharpest and finest. Its three suites are roads, streams, and wanderings. They lead in different directions but collect bits and pieces of consciousness that become an itinerant unity, an image of life.

—MAGNUS RINGGREN, *Upsala Nya Tidning*

"Katarina Frostenson's poems grace like the touch of hand as they simultaneously create the distance that sharpens vision. This manifests through grandiose self-assurance, seriousness, splashes and flickers of joy and wonder that such a thing as language exists."

—TOMAS LÖTHMAN, *Norrländska Socialdemokraten*

"In *The Space of Time* we seem to meet poetry that tries to overpower itself, tease out the essence of its own existence . . . . It is a high point in Frostenson's career. Breathtakingly beautiful, burningly eager. Endeavoring. Dynamic. It is great literature. I can't phrase it in any other way."

—KRISTIAN LUNDBERG, *Östersunds-Posten*

CONTENTS

TRANSLATOR'S NOTE

Så länge språket finns finns du
As long as language exists, you exist

This assertive phrase floats alone upon a paper sea of muted white, on page 101 of Katarina Frostenson's plum-covered collection *Flodtid* (Floodhour; 2011), in the collection's central, 18-page long poem "Orden mot" (Words towards). It was among the first pages I thumbed through when I stumbled upon a row of her colorful books in the Wilson Library at the University of Minnesota as an undergraduate. It's one of those phrases that embeds itself within you as soon as your eyes pass over its letters. It's also one of the few phrases I immediately understood during that first encounter—at least linguistically, having only started learning Swedish several years prior at that point. My interest was greater than my illiteracy.

I remember walking home from the library on that frigid February night in 2016, crossing the wind-blown, snow-soaked bridge that connected the campus's west bank with its east as it stretched over the Mississippi. It was a two-mile walk from the library to my apartment, a half-hour at least.

As I trudged through the snow and slush, those words stirred in my head, inspiring not only thoughts and confusion, but an ineffable conviction. Resoluteness. As long as language was, I was. In that order. Language exists before me, beyond me. In the beginning was the word, we are told. And yet the only words that floated around my mind were those words. I couldn't conjure any of my own, neither spoken out loud into the bleak midwinter air nor silent against the contours of my consciousness. Perhaps that one phrase had forced all others out of my mind, only to be whisked away by the wind, I'm not sure, but what is certain is that I repeated those words over and again on the way home, with different intonations and inflections, with varying pitch and prosody, with revolving rhythm, with and without rhyme or reason, in Swedish and in English. *Så länge språket finns finns du.* "As long as language exists, you exist." Or, word-for-word: "So long language exists exist you."

There are some small but, in my view, deceptively crucial differences between how the sentence works in Swedish and in English. For one thing, unlike English, Swedish grammar enforces strict syntactic inversion where there is a main "anchoring" verb around which other elements move—in this case, *finns du* (exist you). If the clause would stand on its own, it would be *du finns* (you exist). But because this main clause is preceded by a subordinate clause—*så länge språket finns* (as long as language exists)—that entire clause "kicks" the *du* to the other side of *finns*. Thus, *så länge språket finns finns du.* Though, if they themselves were writing the sentence, learners of Swedish would invariably slip up and write or say *så länge språket finns du finns*, which is syntactically incorrect in Swedish but maps onto the word-for-word order of a proper rendering of the sentence in English. "As long as language exists, you exist."

Yet English feels less adamant than the Swedish to me for a few reasons. The first is that there is now no adjacent repetition of *finns* (exist), no side-by-side emphasis uniting language's being with your being. If we abide by the rules of English syntax when transferring this Swedish phrase, language exists and you exist but never the twain shall meet. The second *finns* doesn't vanish, but it does move, it comes later, ever so slightly delayed. It's also worth noting that, despite its existential assertion, this phrase is uniquely intimate, with its apostrophic address. The poem is making a universal claim, yes, but it is speaking to *you*.

The second reason is that there is a comma. There doesn't have to be, but without a comma the phrase feels to me almost flippant. To my mind, the comma helps slow down the rhythm and reinforce the assured register of the line. At the same time, it counterintuitively adds another degree of distance between the clauses, not unlike the separation of the dual *finns*. And while there is no period to close off the sentence, the first word is capitalized—the claim is resolute in its proclamation but leaves itself open to unresolved afterlives.

I could even give a third reason: in Swedish there's no differentiation of verb forms between number or person, unlike English which still maintains a minimal distinction, with more or less variation depending on verb type. I exist, you exist, he/she exists, they exist, we exist. In Swedish, everyone and everything just *finns*, in the same shared conjugation. In terms of Swedish grammar, the existing of language takes the same form as the existing of you, of me, of everyone.

There are some cases where the translator may deem it necessary to bend or break the rules of English grammar to convey what the author is doing in the source language, but this is not one of those cases. Rending English in order to convey a linguistic specificity of Swedish that the poem is not trying to emphasize not only distracts from the point and the power of the phrase but also overdetermines it. Thus, in this instance the best option is for it to be "natural," to recreate the Swedish text's tone in English.

Frankly, this is hardly a typical translation problem. If anything, it's more of a translator's curiosity. It is not one of those infamous "untranslatables." But the reason I mention it is because it gives a sense of the kind of nuance that Katarina Frostenson's poetry explores and is famous for, in both theme and form. In Frostenson's writing, there is no shortage of wonder before language, because "as long as language exists, / you exist."

ɱ

Philosophers have long told us in this or that way that we make and understand our world through our language/s. Some might express this as a matter of limitation, that if we don't have the words for something it doesn't exist. Think Wittgenstein and his most circulated phrase, "the limits of my language mean the limits of my world." Others see language as a matter of revelation, disclosure. Think Heidegger and his mystical predecessors.

If Frostenson has a philosophy of language, it is one that manifests through an attuned attention to how language and world are enfolded within each other and thus both exceed themselves, conjuring a yearning for something more primordial. "[A] language of flesh / all I wished for," as it goes in the closing poem, which also speaks of a yearning to "become / that bareness / the gestures without adhesive, without / syntax // a speech without words yanked out, thrown to the world."

While I doubt any poet would disagree with the sentiment that language, being, and humanity are entangled, Frostenson's poetry puts this into motion by taking this abstract notion and exploring it through the matter of language, by which I don't just mean the paper, ink and glue of the book, but also, and particularly, the substance of the embodied mind that reads and especially speaks the words that come to be represented on the page. For instance, whether explicitly or implicitly, Frostenson's poems often draw attention to how the mouth employs air and muscle to produced contoured sound, be it how the word *imorgon* (tomorrow) decomposes in the poem "Tomorrows" or how the speaker of the poem "Existence" reminds the reader of how children learn to properly pronounce vowels (of which Swedish has nine) in turn encouraging the reader to reflect on, and perhaps also sound out, their own words.

The smallest building blocks of the Swedish language, the otherwise unnoticed minutia of words—especially sounds, especially vowels—are front and center in her poetry. In the history of Swedish poetry, Frostenson's is unique for its primal preoccupation with sound, how sound can make meaning beyond or even without regard to semantics. That it is sound that speaks in and often drives her poetry can perhaps be understood in relation to the notion that language speaks, that we are bespoken by language as it emerges through and animates us. It is thus not surprising that the logic of her poems is often sonic.

At its most innovative, Frostenson's poetry resists recourse to conventional ways of understanding, instead invoking a hermeneutics of the body, of association, of sound. Even if, as critics and scholars have argued, Frostenson's poetry has grown more "accessible" and "open" in recent decades as opposed to her previously difficult and—according to the *Swedish National Encyclopedia*—"hermetic" writing, her tone remains consistent. Some critics describe her writing as serious, mysterious; others as playful, beautiful, graceful. If I myself were to offer a single adjective, it would be: *meditative*. The first definition that appears in my Google search is "relating to or absorbed in meditation or considered thought." Suggested similar words include: *contemplative, prayerful, reflective, musing, pensive, cogitative, rapt, philosophical, wistful*. But it is the word "absorbed" that sticks out to me the most. To be able to meditate, to be able to absorb requires a radical openness to the world, to the flow of space and the flow of time. This is the common denominator of the poems in this book.

In this, I see an affinity between Frostenson and the American poet and critic Lyn Hejinian, whose seminal essay "The Rejection of Closure" expresses many profound resonances with Frostenson's poetry. One shared quality is the preoccupation with the paradoxes that writing poses, which serves as the departure point for Hejinian's text:

> Writing's initial situation, its point of origin, is often characterized and always complicated by opposing impulses

> in the writer and by a seeming dilemma that language creates and then cannot resolve. The writer experiences a conflict between a desire to satisfy a demand for boundedness, for containment and coherence, and a simultaneous desire for free, unhampered access to the world prompting a correspondingly open response to it.

In both theory and practice, the bind that lies at the core of writing is something that the writer must always contend with, through writing. Hejinian's characterization of it in terms of opposing (therefore dynamic, therefore generative) tensions resonates with Carin Franzén's description (see the Afterword) of Frostenson's poetry as exhibiting a dual movement between collection and dispersion, and as aiming to resist the calcification of language in our contemporary age. While Franzén identifies and maps out a poetic deep structure of Frostenson's poetics, Hejinian's specific characterization of the writer's dilemma has helped me to better understand Frostenson's practice. That the tension between boundedness and openness is a key theme of the collection is made more explicit by its original title: *Sånger och formler*, songs and formulae. For Frostenson as for Hejinian, the writer is both blessed and burdened, bound as they are to investigating language with language.

A brief excerpt from this book's predecessor, *Tre vägar* (Three paths; 2013), gives a more concrete sense of Frostenson's own poetics against the backdrop of these abstract notions. She writes that

> poetry does not describe. With its lines it emulates [*efterliknar*] places and peoples and states, there are threads of clearly rendered reality running through, but it is primarily images that poetry writes forth; words bear words, images give birth to new images. They are awoken by sound, from them grows a world that is its own, emerging from the world.

Though the translator is not necessarily beholden to the beliefs of the author, this view of the work of poetry seems to me to lend itself sympathetically to the work of translation. Both are open processes which extend far beyond the supposed finality of the page. Both are phenomenological activities that depend on embodied relationality to (in the case of the author) the world, and (in the case of the translator) as well as the text. The work of writing and translating is that of, to use Frostenson's word, emulation. The poem and the translation are each transformative echoes of experience.

Frostenson herself is a translator, a theme that appears throughout this book alongside odes to philology and etymology. In *Tre vägar* she reflects on the inspiration she received from American poet and artist Jen Bervin, specifically her book *Nets*, a transformative re-writing of Shakespeare's sonnets, in which from the flesh of poetic corpus comes a skeletal extraction, a contemporary poet's interpretation of the vital deep structure of Shakespeare's verse. This leads Frostenson to further reflect not only on the inner workings of poems and poetry collections, but also on the movements of translation:

> Now I'm also thinking of translation, and the powerful dream of being able to pull the song out of the song, out of what one hears, or experiences through the words of the other. Try with a hymn by Hölderlin, read it over and over again until the words sink in underneath and another poem rises up. It can also come quickly, like a flash of lightning from a clear sky, after a single reading: a new, inner poem emerges. An intercepted language, yes, a work of the genius poet that brushes past the text and overtakes the breathing she hears from it. Exhales another song.

The air we inhale is transformed when exhaled. The thing with breathing is that we need, but can never keep, the air we take in. And yet it leaves its mark on our body, and we on its, if it has one. Perhaps it's the same with poetry, certainly so with translation.

ııı

Insofar as translator's notes are to be a space where linguistic challenges are to be discussed, creative choices to be defended, and peace to be made, there are two instances particularly worth bringing up here, since both extend across the collection beyond individual poems.

I mentioned above that Frostenson's poems are often propelled by sonic associations. One such instance appears at the very beginning, in the opening poem "Januaria," where each of the first two stanzas are oriented around a single alliteration: the first with the alliteration of initial /s/ and second with the repetition of the word *här* (here), each marked in the Swedish text below. Each conjures an almost propulsive rhythm (especially in combination with the arrangement of long and short vowels and syllable stress).

Januari, kom med ditt **s**kavande
lätet av **s**aven **s**kruvar **s**ig **s**akta och **s**äkert
upp genom **s**tammen
det enda trädet på gården

barkens allmänord ***här***
vareviga dag, **här** som i **här**d som i **här**da
ett **här**ad

In my English emulation, I found a way to roughly replicate each alliterating ensemble, though to differing levels of proximity to the Swedish. This was easier in the case of the first stanza, where I was able to get six of the seven Swedish /s/'s. Perhaps I could have gotten all of them by using the word "**s**tem" instead of "trunk," but in doing so felt too much of a semantic stretch in this case. I could have also wedged in another /s/ if I strained the reflexive verb *skruva sig* into "**s**quirming it**s**elf," but doing so would seem wonky and overdetermined. Luckily, *läte* became "**s**ound," without the definite article so as to further emphasize the rhythm. (In Swedish, *läte* generally refers not to sound as such—that would be *ljud*—but rather to *how* something sounds, usually in reference to animals.) The alliterative pattern shifts somewhat between Swedish and English but more or less maps on.

> January, come with your **s**craping
> **s**ound of **s**ap **s**quirming **s**lowly and **s**afely
> up through the trunk
> the lone tree in the yard

It was more difficult with the second stanza, where the poem not only repeats sounds but also a word within a word. The wordplay is simultaneously sonic and semantic. In trying to emulate this in English, I had to move farther away from both semantic and sonic proximity in order to approximate both. Whereas Frostenson's Swedish neatly draws attention to how the word 'here' (*här*) is built into other words (***här**d, **här**da, **här**ad*), my English relies instead on both homonym (here, hear) and quasi-heteronym (hearth, hear). It also effectively rewrites the phrase after the comma, rendering explicit and imperative ("hear the harmony") what is implicit in Frostenson's original (i.e. one sees and/or hears the *här* as part of the subsequent words).

> the bark's banal word ***here***
> *every single day,* **here** as in **hearth** as in **hear**
> the **harmony**

The word *här* and the broader theme of place run throughout this collection, and in ways that don't always transfer neatly. For instance, the poem titled "A Neighborhood" in English is called "I ett härad" in the Swedish. A *härad* is an administrative term roughly equivalent to a 'hundred' (in England) or 'county' (in the US), demarcated with stones. The *härad* and its sister term *hundare* (a direct cognate of 'hundred') no longer serve any administrative roles in Sweden. Given that the poem takes place in Stockholm city, where as far as I can tell there has never been a *härad*, I decided to instead use the more obvious word 'neighborhood' in its place. This is but one example of seemingly endless instances of philological, etymological, historical layers to be found in Frostenson's poetry; and the choices that a translator needs to contend with.

The second instance is less about continuity amongst specific lines and more about maintaining continuity across poems. The collection's second section, titled "In the Open" in English, is titled "I vidden" in the Swedish. According to the Swedish Academy's Dictionary, a *vidd* is an "open landscape," often used in the plural (*vidder*). It is also worth mentioning that here Frostenson is again playing with sound, in this case assonance. Throughout the poems in this section words such as ***vide***, ***vid**a*, ***vid***, ***vid**are*, ***vid**eskogar* reoccur, all of which literally resonate with ***vid**den* (the open landscape). Though 'in the open landscape' in a geological sense might be the most literal, its figurative reach extends farther.

As I'm writing this now, my solution of rendering "I vidden" as "In the Open" feels like an almost obvious choice. Yet I recall having struggled over it for a long time. Early drafts of the translation had it as 'In the Void' and 'Expanses.' It didn't start to click for me until Katarina pointed out that the Swedish translation of Austrian writer Arthur Schnitzler's 1911 play *Das weite Land* (translated in English as *The Vast Domain, Undiscovered Land, The Distant Land*) was in Swedish titled *De stora vidderna*, literally 'the great open landscapes.' It seems that for some reason I had been thinking both too literally and too figuratively. Within a few hours of learning about the Swedish title of Schnitzler's play, it occurred to me that "In the Open" was the right rendering. And I began to see resonances that emerged from associations in English and from the broader themes of the collection, and perhaps from also my fondness of Rilke.

The poetic-philosophical notion of "the Open" (*das Offene*) emerges from the Eighth of Rilke's *Duino Elegies*, which begins

> Mit allen Augen sieht die Kreatur
> das Offene. Nur unsre Augen sind
> wie umgekehrt und ganz um sie gestellt
> als Fallen, rings um ihren freien Ausgang.
>
> With every eye the creature gazes
> into the Open. Only our eyes are
> as if reversed, and entirely surround it
> like traps around its free outgoing.

Like much of Rilke's work, the Eighth Elegy has been the object of extensive, sometimes contradictory, commentary by critics, philosophers and literary scholars. What "the Open" is is far from agreed upon, and though I believe that perhaps its conceptual indeterminacy is the very point, there are some generally accepted aspects. Whatever "the Open" is or is not, the Elegy states that it is something borderless that only children and animals have access to. The adult human does not. It could be about nature, about modernity, about apathy, about spirituality, monism, transcendence, reason, knowledge . . . the list goes on. Though there are many spots throughout *The Space of Time* that might point to this affinity with Rilke, it is perhaps in "Siberian Song" where it's most palpable. Adorned with the motif "Two children come wandering in the open [*i vidden*]," the poem tells of two young siblings who try to survive in the wild, *open* tundra of Siberian Russia. However one interprets the finer details of Rilke, if there were ever a context where one could come into contact with such a transcendent state to which "the Open" seems to refer, it would be the one conjured in this poem.

I am not the only one to pick up on this. The prominent Swedish critic Victor Malm contends that her writing "turns" at the millennium from a hermetic skepticism towards the Rilkean "Open." Malm moves beyond taking "the Open" as a matter of poetic mysticism and suggests that for Frostenson it is a necessary attempt to write from perspectives beyond the human or the traditional poetic subject. For Frostenson, "the Open" manifests both in the poetic image and poetic form, and signals a more explicit ecological engagement reminiscent of what American scholar Lynn Keller terms "poetry of the Self-Conscious Anthropocene" which describes the "reflexive, critical, and often anxious awareness of the scale and severity of human effects on the planet." This does not at all mean rejecting the human, but instead attempting to imagine, conceive and consider non-human perspectives in the world. This is most explicit in the poem "Trash Trail," where the reader follows a human hand on its daily trash-tossing. In other words, the openness to the unknown, unfamiliar and unexamined is characteristic of both "the Open" and Frostenson's poetry.

Aside from these loftier ruminations is the question how to render "I vidden" in a way that resonates across the imagined landscapes of the Siberian tundra in "Siberian Song," the remembered cityscapes of "From Minsk," the natural nightscape of "Voicegrass," or the mindscapes of "Marina." Thus the phrase "In the Open" makes sense to me, for a few reasons. One is that it gestures towards familiar figures of speech—if I find myself experiencing some interpersonal tension, I might say something along the lines of *let's just get it out in the open*. It can also conjure notions of wilderness, wide open spaces, and the unknown of the world. It also brings us back to Hejinian and the radical openness of writing, and shows the extent to which even the smallest minutiae of Frostenson's poetry can scale up to the overarching themes of an entire collection.

These examples are representative of the intricacies of Frostenson's writing, and how a small detail can be connected to an entire 'phase' of her career. As a general principle, because I can't replicate every trick or clever phrase that she makes in Swedish, I tried to tease out ambiguities and wordplay whenever I could in English. And without sacrificing sense, I tried to emphasize sound whenever possible.

It's a tired rhetorical trope that things are lost and found in translation—indeed I can admit that my discussion of specific passages might constitute a lost-and-found inventory of language. But it can also be a matter of compensation, of adaptation, of calling and responding across languages, of emulation.

ꟿ

Having worked with these poems off and on for the better part of eight years, I do not pretend that any single one of my translations is 'done,' despite their presence on the page. They are still open, open-ended, in the open.

When, in "Januaria," Frostenson writes of a language that moves forward in time, one that continues to resound, resonate, reverberate into the future, whose words are transformed, that is the work of the poet and the work of the translator.

ꟿ

As Frostenson's poetry has been with me for much of my adult life, there are many people who have likewise come and gone that have influenced my work on these translations, knowingly or unknowingly, directly or indirectly.

First and foremost is Katarina herself, who graciously read many drafts and responded to many questions. I have learned a great deal about the work of poetry and the work of translation through these exchanges.

Though my arrival at and her official departure from the Department of Scandinavian Studies at the University of Washington coincided, Ia Dübois gracefully discussed with me Frostenson's writing, my early attempts at translating it, and my MA thesis on Frostenson's poetry from the 1990s. When I moved into my office in Seattle as a first-year graduate student, one of Ia's well-worn, rubber band-bound folders was waiting for me on my desk, nearly overflowing with decades of research, newspaper clippings and Xerox scans. It has come with me from Seattle to Baltimore to Stockholm to Berlin.

In autumn 2020, I received an email from Enrica Halvorsson inviting me to attend the annual translation workshop *Översättargruvan* on Frostenson's poetry in Hästbäck, Sweden that she co-organized with Elena Balzamo in May 2021. Not only was the weekend itself an incredibly invigorating experience, Enrica also made it possible for me to make the trip from the east coast of the US to the middle of Sweden during a pandemic and through many travel hassles and restrictions. I also want to acknowledge the other participants who shared in the conversations that weekend: Marie-Hélène Archambau, Firat Ceweri, Isabelle Chereau, Daniela Ionescu, Maja Thrane, and Enrico Tiozzo.

As always, there's a host of people who at one point or another, in one way or another, engaged my work with these poems. They include: Amanda Doxtater, Jennifer Gosetti-Ferencei, Kira Josefsson, Marco Pomini, Eleni Theodoropoulos, Rochelle Tobias, Lovisa Wihlborg, and the editors who published some earlier versions of my translations. Thanks also to the people at Kopplin's Coffee in Saint Paul, Minnesota, where I first attempted translating some of these poems (at the table in the corner by the front window).

ווו

In December 2022, Frostenson informed me that the driving force and guiding light behind the *Översättargruvan* initiative, Enrica Hallvorson, had passed away. A remarkable person who fostered a singular space to dwell in and between languages, to bask in their warmth and navigate their borders, Enrica embodied what the soul of translating can be when filled with genuine life shared amongst people, languages, and texts. This translation is dedicated to her memory.

Bradley Harmon
29 April 2024
Stockholm, Sweden

THE SPACE OF TIME

Words flow forth

The sun arrives

No shepherd tends

Everything exists

ADRIFT

Januaria

January, come with your scraping
sound of sap squirming slowly and safely
up through the trunk
                                        the lone tree in the yard

the bark's banal word *here*
every single day, here as in hearth as in hear
the harmony

vague bird voices amongst the branches
chirping in staccato
to hear for the first time in a while
                                                    hear a January day   sparrow!

to dissipate
gentle dispersion and light sifting out through gaps
in the clouds

you can look
you can always look out
                                                                whatever may be out there

a herd of black padded jackets before a row of
letters carcassed onto newspaper headlines
inching sideways, forming patterns

a lattice of language
a noise cage, narrowing hearths, all of it harried
the unfamiliar world at home

sealed up, driven away
to retain and resist images of the *ruined*
to host, not be consumed, not fathom

how the world goes on

a father's gravelly breathpaths, expectoration
belong to leaden days, a distant dejection
the longing unto ash

this month hardens reality
what am I to love here, the question real and unworthy
you groan, mortal

misery you think
the despair of despair
think air instead

as if the simplest thing in the world to say
a single word, durable, like she who taught me to trudge, tug along
smiling, struggling in anguish *turn*

on a dime!
sweet little girl
everything will be fine

exists no more
instead
windy days, a whistling urge to follow the momentum of the moment

and all the while language moves, whipped by the wind, torn into tissue
hastening in the cardinal directions
one with the migratory birds think

to rise is quite simply to persevere
at stages on life's way that coax you to resound
exquisitely, wordlessly, hopelessly

you will still be called song
you who pull the barge, be diligent language   you are on guard
someone must tighten the sail and embrace –

– and since I stood by the willow on the hill
looked out over the valley next to the tracks
as the wires above swung and shivered
sang elegantly in the air – that space
infinite, confined by bending chords, a space
yes that's it, and a capacity – so many words have passed by
in persistently erratic streams
and often an impulse to just break away from it all,
let it lift towards the clouds or sink!
the whole heap of words may go under, time will
take care of that in the end, surely and sorrowfully, but ever since
I stood there by the willow on the hill and looked out over the tracks
    and sensed
a space with your warm rugged
hand upon mine, it was
a first feeling of a future emerging from those words that endure
and evade understanding but still resound that seventh of January long
forward in time

Song Paths

The song arrives
a sure step

the flicker of a fawn on a narrow path
the flare of a fire

a downpour

to be deluged
while standing still

to be pulled back together

I am the path the song takes

amorphous and taut

You, song, can still return long and meandering
like that one time, the first time I saw you

sing for me let it flow
come and crumple

Ariel's song, ding dong
coral tongue
the clock must strike
must get to the core, to the bone of disquiet

revenant
face full of soot and sun
irresistible – come
away with me, leave me on the way

Trash Trail

The hand tosses the item, the hand repeats its gesture each day
tosses away
does it think of the river, the hand thinks
of the hands that will receive

cheese rinds broken combs sunflower seeds
cardboard crayons a big piece of cake carcasses
and nails

by hand, it wastes more than it wants
it ties the bag, walks to the exit
stopped by a voice, like from childhood

                                        where do you think you're going

        the call
mid-gesture, the shadow of a voice of someone left behind

the thought of leftovers
overflowing, all meeting the same fate
everything has to end up somewhere

Magpies on the roof, a woman with a cross braided
into her hair like a dark princess rummaging through the trash bags
sliced through the plastic with her fingers
her hand a seastar in the air
                                                she
vanished, swept around the corner
when a door swung open

a man lugs a fridge out through the door while
spaghetti noodles in the sink
slide silently
down through the pipes
tea leaves follow

feed for the world

the hand touches an unknown item, a round green plastic object among
teabags meat sauce cotton swabs
lemon peels ripped-up postcards paper towels
a faded flamingo

where will you end up

all the things that one just abandons, the hand thinks
mile after mile
after oneself

or that rushes forward like a wave of trash
floating away, transported and sorted *far far away*
in someone else's landscape

that horrible daily happening of
throwing – all the waste you produce
impossible to grasp, with neither hand nor mind, it is

an unfathomable amount

an ancient cell phone at the bottom of the bag
I don't want to see
your sad shell, o you've put in your time, poor thing

amongst carrot peels and plastic, cheese sauce
and envelopes and meeting notes, batteries

if you could come along with us
be flushed through the pipes, kicked around the streets
be crushed, dissolved, burned
carried away with the river

drive to the dumps in the fields
those innocent fields
sink into the furrows, dig down into the crops
become feed for the livestock

be rejected everything must be taken care of –

Bread thrown out, stale *Brot* right
before our eyes
we stood, with fallen hands, as so often happens in existence, muted
before the daily bread stuffed into black bags

a child tried to crush an expired loaf
too old, alas
inedible
"soon I'll be whisked away"

a pile taken by hand
to be driven to the animals
to be kicked around
grounded down by mute jaws, the bread
our daily shall be sliced with reverence
taken by hand and cherished
to the last lump
the swelling of shame – the words are expired

since "it's a waste of time"
to cry over the spill
everything must disappear
depart via underpasses or the most
tangible trails

be ground up, sanded down or stranded around in the meadows
and gently decay

– obsessively following the green plastic thing's journey
how it's pushed through pipes and rafted on rivers
washed into the sea
just to get stuck under an island in the middle of a storm, one might imagine
in the animal's throat
how it's broken down so slowly

it will return

it will become something else

be transformed how

far away the troll tends the fire

Thinking of Ostia, the debris on the beach where the poet lay battered
Il pianto della scavatrice, traces of the trail, grass burned yellow and piles of
reeking remains
and now the lamb that crowns the garbage pile in Acerra!

there is no circulation, everything must shore up, almost everything
must be handled by other hands
be burned, poisoned

or stored in the fields

everything must be taken care of

everything has to go somewhere

who sits at the final destination
and cooks down the soup
into seafood

all this plastic you have on your conscious

a ship comes loaded, soon an armada
to the land of India where brown-legged boys on the hunt for metal
rush at breakneck speed amongst piles of tangled nets, reclaiming from
the rubbish
cheering in the joy of a string
rejoicing in recycling

man is witty
but ultimately outwitted, her hands burned, the structure
overpowers

the sinister order rolls out its tarpaulin
a cover
its way across the seas
of rageful fish, overflow of capital, coasts where seabirds hang

over the cliffs on plastic strings
and new landscapes
of appliances, mountains of fridges and freezers
o silhouettes

glaciers that truly never melt
a *new perpetuity*

a new kind of iceberg
denser, more glowing
entirely un-meltable

in transit to Ghana, from the roar of fridges rocking the seas and scraping
against each other

the song of the appliances

remorse – what happened to that word, the hiss in the throat and
peace pulled out with the root

everything has to end up somewhere
to be handled by darker hands
ending up embedded in fields
stored by someone else

the ants take care of their waste and bury themselves
in the trenches
break it all down together, so intelligently

let us be ants

or return as birds
travel back

recycling, the word's small buoyant movements

sorting amongst the word-roots

it has been rediscovered

what has?
the beach where the waste waits

resting in an eternal landfill

until the wave
the troll's sauce simmers

you will wake up one day in a landscape overflowing
you will stand in the flood
you will hardly have time to think
you will look at your hand
you will say *hand*

everything has to end up somewhere

and everything must return

you will not sink
not go under
you will wade forward
stand in the filth
hear it scrape, drip, sputter

it will not burn
down, it will last forever

Turn

Never so many noes as today
it is the day of Lenz – January 20th everything turns here
I say
                                        wind, sweep across the canopy
fields and trees into a flame
rush to where I stand in the avenue
                                                                                the flame encroaches

what will it steal?
everything, everything I was
nostrils eyebrows
forehead earlobes
speech, it will steal all speech
it will steal everything

buried in a Bruegel-gray, vigil
as the soul turns its body up and down
only the facade remains *face*

with no face
bewildered is the one who wanders without qualities
one with the houses, the roofs, the windows, corners, backs
cobblestones and in a word   patience

Silent Directive

See and go

All that emerges can be seen

To see without succumbing – is the path

to see and leave, a silent stream of this and that
tree trunk sandbox gravel trails
a coiled branch

the shining tree

empty days. You entrance me. Let me feel this
as I receive it

Pilot light
luminous words
snap, step, metal roofs and clouds

the street is a structure that calms
layer upon layer of facades and glass
to the suburbs and back again

Hägersten is a kangaroo pouch in thought
bearing, brown, damp
turning in and out

like the words: you birthed me mother

listen: there is no going back

—

Wake, awake

A rain drew in during the night. The night rain pulling a membrane across the objects. Muffled sounds

Thumb on the back of a chair, finger on a cork. Listless and
lamentful and the cracked skin under your foot
Insufficient

I am insufficient
it will suffice
it is more than enough to be

it is always sufficient to just carry on
still, still
still the words sing eternally *it is not enough*
to wake up, to conjure a voice

Take the word night seriously, heave
it like a cloak over your body
linger long enough that it shields your eyes
that it blackens your entire vision and
you must rise for the sake of rising
and to not suffocate
                    one must always rise higher

Write so that you rejoice and fly high
the sound of galloping hooves. Spark

Linger in a space with Marina Tsvetaeva and Birger Sjöberg
Feel the current of language

The crosspollination, the meeting of the unfamiliar
So that you again get a feel for what language can be

Always remember what language can be
Speak not. Do. For
the language of poetry may be dying. Nettles, the sprawl, the amorphous
springing forth, searching with snout and scent across the earth

the mundane remains, a voice says resist

By force must the song be written

—

Sing anyway

All that sings, sings for the second time

Nausea, you feel the loathful wave
again
the emphatic chatter and power of the progression, still it persists

The song is a trawl, pulling backwards

The song is an arrow, it aims

Draw the bow of song

The gravitation itself, the barge   yes
no against
the resistance to the song feeds it
what we know well, beyond and before

what we not yet know, the song
going on its way, the last that leaves the body is

the song from sense

My being. The song is my being.

—

How long will it take

A voice-net loosens, pulls through the night, to the hearths out there
A net wants to trawl whatever may appear

A word, nothing more, the night is here
Syria, infusing, is the night

a coal-black veil covering all
Kobanî

hearths

a single name can expose everything   you see the devastation in just
the names

Syria
Kobanî

the chasm

to sing of others
to sing can be to take over

How should I
say
speak
think

The thought is a prayer, it moves silently outwards

Sense, seek out a nest
it is impossible without connection
find your sister

a sister in Syria

thought twines the thread

a night sister
a sentinel

she bears a history
scorched earth

she points to the selion, the soil, where I will go and wait, see
lay out words one by one, but no song there, none

Disappearances

You lift off from the word
what else could get you to rise
other than the sound of swift wind   maybe
may be
                                        a sail tows towards the market

culling forward like usual across Sergels Torg, your face
among faces, sucked into the sound of headphones
so forlorn with the cords across your cheeks

the white lines through which speech flows
never-ending languishing language – an intangible world
I want your letters, fingertips
and eyes that open on contact

maybe the gust of another
reaches you, opens your face with a puff
of exhaling sound *may be   can just arrive like*
a light from your eyes

Reed, world, thinking
                                        that thought becomes kindling
crumpled up in haste
what remains of the world but momentum

to be overwhelmed by the feeling of grasping a fragment
of the ineffable

to be bypassed by that which need not be comprehended
for hands have ceased to function out there
you will soon pay with your lifelines

the body the silent being
at the center of it all

the text lies in another time
that is this mysterious feeling

At January's end an old face
enchanted by the snow
                                        for the last time under the flakes
trickling in its furrows
                                        melted by sunshine   old girl

am I in your way

the question vanishes from earth
a world expired
                                        you gentle time

I mumble the formula for a disappearance
a place emerged from where you stood and
you are nowhere to be found

A Neighborhood

What is here called? the question hovers
I know where I am, but what kind of place is it – *this is a neighborhood*
thought answers, sweeping around the corner

Sveavägen – how linear you are
I ought to love you, from end to end
If you bore borders and wreaths, framed by other words

we could ride along on horseback at night
the street's silent *here*, in a neighborhood
where names stand like shields, Ignis, Ica, Seven Eleven

but the street's name, thought whispers, could it be

Disintegrated

dispersed and devastated, this stretch of street where
anything can be prey without warning, the laws changed by the fear
of being flooded with smiles, harassed

harrying hosts, here has become a camp
piles of packaging and scraps, as you sweep around the corner comes
the scent of soil, below the Ignis butterfly

think, behind every person a world, an entire *here*
a background, a house left behind
paths, furniture, scythes and sickles

the blue armchair someone left out for the hibernators
seems as if drawn by horse, pushed by a wave – a street
is not a river but it can remind of one

the shipwreck, the world, the floating raft

and so she sits there in the day's flood
with her already crackled wind-bitten face
staring straight out into the day

with nothing to say, a toe, like a root
peeks out from under the hemline
I reach down and lose my balance

a sign of the cross

smiles encircling each other

an ache of syllables, no song from the camps along the road
as far away as I could hear that winter
the song has died within our bodies, hardened and calloused

someone harvests oats in complete silence
here in this neighborhood

where Right – the question of what the right thing is to do
or not wreaks havoc on the senses, across the nerves
sleeps and arises

is inaction *legal* – who commands the corners, who
belongs and doesn't, what is separated from knowledge and for how long
can poverty last

I set the limit for what I give each day
what others, and which of them, are worth
to not belong and still stay put is existence –

sense wants to vanish, flee from vacillation

give me a sign, a solution, a law
there is no right answer, thought answers and disappears
out the door, one's own haven

there is only the day's bread
to be here on this generic day every single day
in the eternal conflict zone

the brown dome below the precipice calms for a moment
my gaze rests –
upon the soonest sight of Stadsbiblioteket time opens up

the wondrous rotunda against the sky, the willow trees
the hill and the archer
the firmament above – the openness

you can sweep around it in a different way
than everything else here
get a temporary vertigo from it

mother with her dark hair, in her suede jacket running towards the gate
up into a hug, her swift smile summons light
reflections along the street, a medieval sun settles on the road

can you sense the scent of wisdom wafting from her, it was then and
it is here

that is home, among camps of strangers
and there she stands in the middle of the road with her crackling
black Madonna face as if out in the fields

a plot of Romanian land, the most stunning neighborhood imaginable with
poppies and horses, a barley-blue sky
she calls out *mama*

the sky blushes at the end of the street

the man who sleeps in the doorway across the street from us
under his hood, I never see his face
we sleep as if in parallel

I see him set up his camp each night at the same time, a blue
cocoon to wrap around his body
next to the pot someone carried out from a house with a bright kitchen

the condition: exposure
perhaps he sings his body to sleep
under the covers under the snow in a foreign neighborhood

flakes fall evenly
the same snow settling on everyone
eventually something arrives that resembles sleep – white lines

Mania/Lines

Line, the word exerts a pull
the thought of being drawn out to the end

the string wants to be tightened
nerves must be strung, they seek their ache
                                        whirring is the nerves' song
we are on our way to the end, but – there

the red lines of the nerve atlas are so elegant
many miles of you are within me
if you unravel
                                        become a bird formation –

we want to incinerate in the air
we want to be lines
our impulse is to be c o n s u m e d

                                                            symmetry shall have soul's breath
                                                            symmetry will be my death

Anguish, here you do not belong
in the long
                    gray, languishing thread
how does everything become constraint

this mournful control I
have begun to exercise over my being
must be exorcised at all costs

driven off the stage
                                                            disappear
a triumph, to be entirely beyond compare

think in slightly holier and happier ways
instead
to approach the great ineffable is a wonderful charge

to be simply enchanted by light
a rare commodity
                              no the opposite

What is it that sounds of fingers
bringing forth Bach
an infinity
how it echoes, and therefore so haunting how it just ends
fades out
freezes mid-line in the Contrapunctus 14
                                                            that's how it was, everything halted
in mid-breath   grasp the bed frame
the room turned upside down
                                                            in the seconds when you
died
with a firm grip on another's arm
flow my tears and take my grief with you
listen to that which continues to resonate
within the body beyond all speech

                                                                notes are the bones that sing

The Brook – Song

– that I writhed
in the panic of being bound
                                        it was early

like an eel twisting *in the memory of sense*
the body – a box
                              through which it will flow
the transition itself

the basin inside
sinker lead frames container

the human stands up
she moves forward
thanks to her pelvis

so outstanding   to be able to stand
set off push forward and away

the instinct to hunt, the urge to flee   I love you dear brook
you who get me to move
                                        homo nomadus

where dance was borne, everything echoes
impulse flows
like a child at unbridled play but

water can stiffen

the jaws' equal, the bite
and the pelvis
parallel centers of unblessed spirit

that was what happened, when one lay there without words
to be held tight against one's will
an indominable infant
how easily a child can slip away

what holds you is the terror
of being held tight, small eels
                                        slunk across the table

the brook the fear
of falling

touch me not and
touch me
yes water can stiffen, that would be unfortunate

spin me around and twist all that surrounds
all the river wants is its outlet, to run

to lie like Moses in the reeds, in any which way
wrapped in brown
in Beuys' wax and feel
a longstanding yearning
to pursue

to get up one day in peace   o eventually I will get you to flow
circulate blaze become
running water again
fleeing

The Space of Time

Where does time end up?

it goes up in smoke
it just twirls around
it lays down at the center of space
curled up, a snake

we stand and stare before the question – sheep in the field – at something in between us

as if space holds our time within itself
our life *now perished*

the lived shall have its place
it demands its space
surely it has to be somewhere
all the time that has passed

who stands there in the ring
no one
there is no one

no sinkhole either
                    everything is separate

—

Far away – the feeling
of nearness – *kenne ich nicht*

but the sound of your movement
in its abrupt arrival
perhaps a paw that brushes across a cheek
for contact is a paw
the feeling of lightness
but most of all the gaze that traverses the distance
longing – a thread
turning and trembling and
pulling back, beloved string

and how you move so as not to disturb
that which is called dance – graceful steps

in a flash we stand there hushed in the middle of the room

never hinder one another, give – space

there are three of us

you, me and lived time

where do our embraces dwell
in the inner
that realm

        have I become virtual

time wants us to look at it

—

But if my love
. . . inexplicable creature . . .

is not a line that leaps out of me, not a stream
or flood
but i n f a c t resides in small pieces of everything
in many places, lingering strewn about everywhere
fringes and flecks

what is a pattern
that which breaks apart and assembles anew
just look at the puzzle
across the floor when all the pieces are scattered   Si!
there they lie and an image
exists in the middle of it all

—

One time we studied each other's hands
looked up and smiled and we agreed:
parallel lines, running side by side

—

Your back stretches out
time extends with me
for how long have I watched it, how many miles –
there's no way to go through, it lies where it lies
a limit, and you are there, there behind
within?

we are what always becomes in that space
where nothing arrives

—

Why do you get up and
run away from me
it is to save us yet again
with distance

and longing must return to its burrow in the mountains, to the cavern
to high up below the mount of heaven, in the void
perhaps here is where time dwells after all

we have dissolved

Our life is about to capsize
into a volta, what am I saying
over the edge

the shadowsnake down there in the slump may devour
and forge ahead with us
we will be brought along in parallel
where the lines *meet*

doesn't exist

but further out

There there

A broken piece
a beloved thing
repair it, let it be

a corner
the emptiness where someone sat
close your eyes, embrace the space

a rickety table
chipped legs
the tiny squirrel in the spruce

a stained hand
a wrinkled cheek
muted throat

brown, skewed, cracked, empty and rare
everything is breaking down
beloved blemishes

Tomorrows

Tomorrow I will creep out in a forest
and set myself against a tree, then after a while
curl around it
Gnawing on a piece
of bark tasting the warmth
my teeth go through porous layers
I am nourished
by air
o let it
go
words flow down
my whole body soon envelops the trunk
I am in my element, shrub and pine
a roe comes to observe
we are the only ones here
it is called solitude and it is not demise
petite roe, its great gaze, linger not, go to the glade's light
I graze upon it, tranquilly
everyone's dream, to disappear in peace
on the bare earth
wither, near the reality
of the word. Tomorrow. To morrow   w rm t

IN THE OPEN

Voicegrass

Voicegrass

the word the night bore
pulled you out of bed

perhaps the memory of Gullberg
the grass sings for feet astray

a flock out there, voices of the dead woven
without sound like the growth of grass

I am your carpet where you tread

The Street's Name

It lies there in the light of day
faintly ruffled by its name
someone says it and continues on

someone says it and comes home

a rose rests outside a gate
one day someone thinks without words a face

the street's name, recited in stone
someone walks on it, stirs up dust

a name
what is a name
the immortal crown that remains
a set of syllables (once t h a t p e r s o n)

someone said it for ten years
someone called it out
someone wrote it down, no image appeared
and then one day when walking past
the name ran across their lips
and at first there were only sounds, spoken aloud

e l s a b r ä n d s t r ö m s g a t a
i n f r u ä n g e n

a stream of light unfolded
a ruffled strand of hair

someone said it again
and someone else passed by with the clouds

like the body of the poem before the words arrive
like the story that takes place
like how everything is and must be awoken time and again

in sunlight and dust
a women on a path
in the time of war

the Angel of Siberia
on the gravel's road
meadows of death

she was a light, a link

what is a name
a rose unfolded

what is a syllable, what is a human

someone says it and leaves
someone says it and comes home
someone says it and the street's name bursts forth

and the sunlight
and the gravel glow
a woman's life
and all that existed
in the time of war
a sea of names

Siberian Song

Two children come wandering in the open

Night, no sleep

all under heaven is given
to thought

if the tree of sleep does not exist
up which one can climb, find a nest and go dormant
with arms around the trunk

but where do they all go, those in the army who wander
between the walls with bread in their hands
milk behind their lips

and who dream of lines, of disappearing
to a land without a name

all of us who haven't been able to sleep for years
are out wandering through night and through thought

would rather be in other places

in the legs of the seaman, in the blue of his trousers

in the oak forests

in the room where Rimbaud and his mother quarreled

in the sea
where whales turn to the deep

in the resonance of throat singing

night, no sleep

Siberia is given to thought
Katinka

among the goldfinches

willow

prunes and prey

where two children come wandering on the path

call them in

those two
who emerged from the belly of an airplane
in the middle of a Siberian forest

my lambs
I count you off: one two

you who wander in the open

twin berries, equal unto despair

if sleep never arrives
you will walk on endlessly this winter

you who stood by the shed
in the yard
with short-cut hair
hands caressing baby birds
stern and sore
Russian youths

you who laugh at all concern

colored by ink
small soldiers
traversing the tundra

the plane
took to the trees
the pine crowns collapsed, the body broken in two
a rain of objects across the entire forest

all the small catastrophes that exist
that vanish into the open
how can
catastrophe calm sleep
during a night in the northern hemisphere

I think
about how
you crawled out of the body of a plane
out of a gray cocoon
like a birth to the open
and went dormant

the miracle that we exist at the same time and under the same sky
that a few lines rattle the night
two siblings survive plane crash in Siberia

no other witnesses, no
the birch rounds are always a witness
did you see the eyes sister, the black ones, there in the darkness
there are wolves in Siberia

you got up and moved on
did not look back, to see if it was still there
and it was, mother's body

it was much later that words came
accompanied by sorrow

you walk on the path
and you do not sing

one with the trunks
with the forest paths, invisible
two small trunks walking alone
siblings from Sakhalin

di to – the poor
gray-eyed, tattered

no seasons whatsoever
Si Si Siberian spring
pure time measured by birdsong, among the starlings

and the redpoll

the flock of goldfinches

as if borne from the body of a plane
slippery and gray like her hands

there is no one
no one else in the entire open
you are borne
into survival

so go and graze the wood sorrel on the way
do you see the glade sister, the twin neighbor

further, we go further, eat rummage graze
spruce shoots
blackthorns and crowberries, if there are
crowberries in Siberia, everything exists

we will live, search for lycophytes to place on our wounds
we will heal
ensnare a hare, a little brother
make a fire   survive
we have survived! we will

eat prunes
if there are now prunes in Siberia
everything exists
in Siberia
wild brown prunes
yellow in flesh
to bite in with small white teeth
so they burst
wrinkled like cheeks, an old woman
with straw that tickles the mouth

and everywhere her face and the words *this is not enough*
she exists no more, the open exists

onward my lambs, one two
a pair of eyes
nearby in the dark
by the foot of the mountains where the black diamonds are
where one sleeps at the base of a tree

in the open, if the open still exists in Siberia
of course there are willow forests, wide willow forests
wolves, tigers – the children sleep now
soon they will sleep but not yet

shall we starve foxes
with bark, build boats
fell tall trees with our own hands
travel on them

they paddle over the great river Lena
parentless they swim like beavers rolling in the mud
river siblings, prune siblings
Siberia siblings

children of the forest
are you lost, not
children of the open
equally pale
under the willow
you are unseen

the fire smokes
the smoke sleeps
both hum

soon in space   with that dog
the stars that wander in green

the song is the cocoon
because it never ceases never closes, the song belongs
to the siblings

Siblings

Siblings
banging each other's heads
hard enough to make thunder roar
and sparks soar

the s t a r s s c a t t e r

elbows thrust to the gut, right where it hurts, directing force
with a smile
trapping, testing and teasing

for siblings tread into each other's territory
infiltrate each other's circles
resemble one another, want to be separate

siblings wander
scatter into the void
hardly even remember one another for long stretches of time
and are brought together when they don't expect or want it
for

siblings are planets
pulled into the same orbit
sewn together by strings
united by blood and flesh

grown-up siblings who once pulled each other's hair
stitched up the slices on their knees
hurt on purpose

threw each other's things and destroyed gleefully
tilting over worn-out items
tearfully eating from the departed's breakfast bowls
collecting tablecloths, cords
dragging the trash left behind

entwined, for siblings are a flock
yes, they are small wolves

testing teasing
the rest of it under the rug, for to be a sibling is to let live, save for
the fights and eyes like suns

Marina

Sung into the slot

sun and dust

it streams out and meets the rain

becomes a river

all the river wants is a way out

is that all   yes that's all
over and over
collapsed and continued
Marina

repels me and delights

Tsvetaeva
the name rends and bends
it resists

Repelling
an incessant struggle against the emphasis of song
love it
                    its *sturdy secret*

who pulls the strings   no one knows

the silken horsehair of longing! sunbeams and golden hair
being pulled back by the rope black as night as the loneliness
in all that exists

Marina, you can be addressed
contested
warrioress and interlocuter

a gust
not rescuing but remaining, debilitatingly indispensable

disruptive and necessary
(and is that not
the same thing)

annunciating
stern and unlettered

yes, the poems – must bend back around
and barge in, continue their marionette dance

(it is mania
but it is more –)

where steps can fall so gently, yes step by step
win what you said
nakedness

what goes on
with neutral *pas*
and makes the conditions clear

leaving its pupae
in the depths of the sea

Just see and record what appears, write it
down
it is hearing – soundwaves – that makes sure that the poem
always heels

or a defect
perhaps – a tic?

something collapsed I carry
wings turned towards the heart

I have foundered
my entire self

cannot be helped, must be *ex ex* expressed
and be resisted? Yes!

the poet's wet dream to tread with even steps
set down her foot, not see the toe that flutters
the heel that refuses to meet the ground here but
somewhere else
impatience   you are my impulse

when man used to stand like a child artless in a field
and just be, look on, record what was seen

what appears

how sound arrives   sound

the gust blows again

it grows wings and carries off

wings conjugated by silence

I come across the Marina biography on my way into town
the eye-deafening image of her on the cover
I had forgotten that you wrote the forward, Birgitta
The words strong, as if they wanted to take themselves out of language
to grab me by the nose
catch my eyes, knock out my teeth
I sit at the Piccolino cafe and observe the autumn leaves
when the sun breaks out and shines through them as the wind takes them
into the air and around the whole park
October gold
life my sister
want to drink wine wine wine
disappear into that frightening beaming face
on Slottsbacken Russians stand in grey caps and rose-gray blouses
I wonder which senses Marina dwells in here, hopefully with someone

Marina October apple astrakhan
the words beloved beloved beloved
helmet of hair beaming black, within it every color and sheen
the rainbow
the painful bow, the song
how could you rhyme everything
how did you not fall apart sooner
you are virtually the only thing in my thoughts these days
your existence – o how it morphed, the sound of rails, of hooves,
exuberance
the silent rooms, noose
language's inner friction and abrasion
how it summons sound and lifts
And the meager light. Striations. You wrote that joy is:
"A desk of one's own. The health of my dearest. Whatever weather.
And freedom."

Must one still sign up for the Mountain? And Forever?!
(when one can go to the edge of sense, stand before the simple line)
Rage
                    End in the void   flailing
broken

Begin and End for evermore
burn and simmer

to re-form sound

speak for the first time

intonation
inhalation

stab the air in search of – flesh
this hunger for *sound*

out of an emptiness

what was it he said, Sergey Efron
a mighty oven that craves wood, wood, and more wood
so she was

one cannot like you, only obsess over you, trepidatiously turn
to you

until the howl
again

from the fantastic impulse to excavate sound
throw up, carve out
the word and cast the carcass to the scavenger

which is perhaps hate, or something

the impulse to Begin

o now I think of the children wandering across the open

in great motherlessness

to sound once more

to recreate the universe
through her

so that She awakens in the open
in the gravel in the storm

and appears patiently noble
divinely dissatisfied

there is a twig in the great white
it is you you you

you smile
the most skewed of smiles
and the cruelest tenderest

it is a game to write, and in bloody seriousness, danger
ash
green
steps far away

There is a forest
and within it a heart – *viscera*

for days on end, I can take root among the branches-signs
unknown

explore Russian with an ax
reach into it – break it open

in order to reach *It*

the text laughs – a witch – when one
attempts an approach

see a light cross over the road

the lines of the air-poem

sound

shimmering

Hear me now
Cease my sounds

Marina

From Minsk

Minsk, min, skatt, sss

the name
            sun-feather

a creature, pewter-gray white
emerges from the giant Menesk

the name *Minsk*

looming largely
ineffable city
monstrous in the backlight

see a city
only from afar
always from afar
                                    there lies Minsk
a stage at its center

an enclave as its landscape

see from a distance, how it ascends
that says it all, you will not enter here

it might as well be a wall
die Stadt M

we venture into a city where everything is exposed
and nothing is seen

in the white light blinding mutely but
a circus!
golden, red, a circle of bright light on the way into Minsk!
so there is life after all

parks and squares, an all-consuming regularity
the boulevard

we stepped out of our bus as if in fear
stood in a square

to stand in a square here is
to be seen from all directions

to walk across it
to wait for the shot
a desire to go underground
where does one disappear to here
in Minsk

there is no shadow
there is only one color out here
pewter-white gray

we took to a space where everything, in contrast, was brown
as if silenced by the earth
with a name like the star, *Iska*
the wandering

it was for your sake we came here to
great squares without shadows
to translucency
to a river under ground
we drank horseradish schnapps

ate minced raw meat, a runny white egg yolk·
Minsk gave me anosmia
a year without smell, like a foretaste of memory loss
it's certainly not Minsk's fault that viruses exist but
a metallic smell that detracts from all scent emanated from there
as if numbed, deprived of connection
it is an unreality to not sense smell

as if to not exist
a threat
by the name of Minsk

anonymity

always a stage
like nowhere else in the Kyivan Rus
with rivers to the Bothnian and Black Seas, connected
but closed
an ash

do not open the memory of Minsk
Iska
of your name that vanished on the way away

for a moment a form hovers above the square
a tail of Chagall, a comet
it was blue
and there was the circus, a child's joyous cry!
hovering like starlings from the beyond, in the air of Polesia

and the herons, the roads without end
the lakes, the water no one sees
there is a river in Minsk, it is buried under stone
Njamiha, the river of sleeplessness

it was buried down under ground
subterranean, a slain river
it says everything

like the bodies, the ground trembles
across the pits in Minsk
a memorial garden now
every name

Minsk, an ash
do not open your memory Iska
to what you became
your root, your mother, your white rose
went to Der Bund and wandered off, probably sensing a scent
of what was to come

that is:

Iska from Minsk
vanished from Belarus
through Poland and down to la France
became Cécile
tried first with the Kingdom of Sweden, not allowed to enter
wasn't welcome, such things are handed down
from mother to son and so on to the next link

sewed
without woe, silenced
the name vanished, switched out

survival
the ground trembled for days afterward
by the bodies thrown down alive

the city of abyss
the city of wolves

if she had stayed, you wouldn't exist, my Minsk, everything depends
on Iska
as Cécile escaping the pit in Minsk

here one is as if mute, I say loudly
an undying atmosphere of anticipation, a threat

what I know of Minsk is what I see, a stage wide open
closed
and the star above the ghetto, gold on the brown-green map
over Die Stadt
a phantom
from outside, not a trace, the pain that wanders from branch to branch
foot to leg, from son to son
and out into the ether

min skatt

Minsk will not depart my sense
it is branded white

We walk through a square a group of people a shadow
falls over us
the giant Menesk
he, the gray
wolf's man

here there are few visible words
those that exist loom large
like a threat

no river but
the memory of a river

and a blue form looms in the distance

city with neck irons
the beginnings of your days

your root unearthed, the white sorrow
visible in your face, the rootlessness lives on
in your son, in everyone

your origins
Minsk
min skatt
oblivion
the wanderers

no one is remembered there
there is no trace
only your face, some features
a weak airing-out of

earth and the memory of the bodies
a pit never more
not a single image from here
mother Iska Cécile root
the word Jew
ambling
white sun
sea, no sea
land
enclave

min skatt
itself buried in the word Minsk
looming – white
pewter-white city

Heron Lands

Grain and sky

Cornfield   flatland

Gray houses in a dream
Brain-barns

Weeds growing in the ditch

The fence green, beautifully carved far away so turquoise

Few flowers, starving out the sandy earth
flowers are considered frivolous

Sparsely populated

Lonely trees. One with pears
Pears are called hrúša
a soft tongue, Belarusian

the word FOG alone in the fog
a truly thick one as the nightingale's song breaks through
the bird roars, falls from infarct to the ground

Fog Cloud
unseen
Heron Lands
The black genus hides out in the swamps

roads do not bend here
they stretch on into endlessness
a glimpse of the blue tractor

a pink gate

a remote land

and the forests
the moss
the poison in the sorrel
tears shivering over springtime soup

what can I eat
where can I be
can I lie in the grass
quiet anxiety
life-threatening for humans

can this landscape heal
can it be itself again
and can humans return
see a child's swing

never do the roads bend as they cut through the heron lands it is
a straight stretch into eternity and out into even sky

eleven thousand lakes lie in this landscape
none are visible but farther in the distance runs a river named Pina
lies a city named Lida
a land that is a land that is no land to be remembered
long straight roads that never seem to turn
the monotony from which song must eventually rise
to the delight of the poet

SORROW PATHS

Existence

Existence: pronounced *ex ist ence*
an exhalation, the word grew luminous and long
it laid itself before my toes, spread its flame forward, farther out
it was a laterna, a carriage carrying
the word through the dark
along the sidewalks
the word e x i s t e n c e
the leaves had begun to golden
the street dampened and blemished
it was October already
a month without a frame

extended: now it begins, the extended
light passes away

The cold
When it arrives
To disappear at night
Wind
Without sense
Settle on the orange blanket

And the snowy expanse out there
Look out without looking as if
an unobstructed outlook
Nothing can happen in the bitter cold

Only the speech from calm hands
Cast out lines
Like the language of a thing
cliffs – expanses
To let it last not pull
your breath in before the end
Then in long stretches let the rhythm stretch to Sakalin
where it continues on into loneliness   isthmus

Like how leaves rustle
a child's vowels sound
the swirling of the air
and the stillness of everything else
to go on
how do you do it
we say: stand up
push forward like a little creature day in day out

A head tucked in
taken care of
cradled, carried away by horse and carriage
Rest in a pen with the head of a napping calf in your lap, a little itchy
just as well
straw is straw

Fall not into rhythm
coax the lullaby
to tenderly dismantle form, how do you do it
you just let it go
go language go

like a Beuys melody
a stranger humming along   ne ne
yes yes ne ne yes

My face in my hands
for the first time
pronounce *pater*
the spacious lines
the Symmetry
Teach me how to hold myself inside
the edges

Like a bear almost, paws lifted
toward the sky

I cannot feel the yoke
The air is light and damp
as if full of wet whiskers, brushes
beloved November
Darkness a cradle
Writing in shadow
letters become peripheral
wobbling as they come forth, *now they are letters*
what grace, these days merely pass by
nothing else to say
nothing else to carry

I go to mom with coffee and a lamp
It's so dark in here
Where is she about to set off to
no one can say
not even her anymore
I leave and remember Anita Björk
austerely starry-eyed, slightly fox-like
Tintomara
Careful harsh lovely old women
Longing for Lund
for your capacious hands
for the pensive gaze only you had
How you could look out and just be, for so long, as if under water

I write in the dark
transfer lines

a tongue not speaking
but sustaining
pray and prey are two words here
both of reality, of the same sound
she who prays for me preys on me, and vice versa

The low tones
and the words *come to me*
my yoke is gentle
You should not carry others, that is a moral
what should you do otherwise
what should you do in the meantime
Stand aside, follow, falter not

Search
for the delightful bedwarmth
I am not homeless
I consider myself grateful
the traffic goes as it goes, just goes on
there is a kind of security in hearing its rumble
someone coughs outside my window
a room lights up across the street. The foreign world at home.

and the word that gets me to get up in the morning
and the thought of her
still lingers out there somewhere
but when my mother no longer exists
I will sink into unreality
so it must be
is there a language for that
there must be

A cluster of people clad in black stood in a darkened stairwell
like an image from Dagerman's *A Burnt Child*, how one descends
the stairs into sorrow. They had buried a mother. Tears beneath
their words

I tiptoe towards your end

stay silent and run wild

the best thing about this time is being able to grasp the edges of being

where the small things matter and the truly great

Heaven, she answers! She answers today, too

the sisters are stricken with fear

sisters fumble
and flail

what is our direction without her
do we tumble into a sea
carelessly

and this I said to you, my sister, when we walked in the square in Tumba
that we are probably loveless, we feel troubled – sometimes
almost angered by being put into service
by being taken out of time by time. Noli me tangere dear family. And then
the guilt, and complaisance. And so warmth and care
streaming endlessly

grief and care

She abides
so softly
those unknown spaces
tears that cannot be halted
She continues to see everything
that can be seen in there
Patterns, colors, skies, sides, squares
she pays attention to movements, especially ways to move on
this I've inherited from her
she shows me with her hand, draws
with gestures, the wave, smiles
things emerge. Their gestalt. Their forms. Nothing escapes

Sorrow and fear. Rain in the air

Now we go on. We can't go. Now we go

A Tuesday in November and it's raining. It is a day that
will never come again. Tuesday the 27th of November, it
rained all night and all day long. Long long song. 24 hours
of rain. A true rainy day. One should be grateful

Grain

The fragility of the tree. The stillness of everything. *My soul my companion*

Stamina. The quiet smolder, *scorching* at my knee

The world speaks nonetheless. High and low, endeared existence

Titles light up the day here. "Joy and Asymmetry"
and "im felderlatein." The poets Rekola and Seiler. Like
brethren in being

Friendship reproduces faith

Faith. The word conjures a pair of shoes. And trails to tread, roots that
anchor

Trail, a simple interior word
Engraved in memory. For it now seems that
these paths are missing. And now they must be summoned:

Tolerance. Bedwarmth. Body to body
Dry clear climate

Wishlist. Soft and hard
Something touches me, tugs at my hair. Says you *exist*. And
is merciful to me

To accept the world is noble. To not do so is something else

Let time go so it will come back
The small stamina. The little flame. The kettle

Thank you for your existence, she said quietly
Did she mean – reliability?

I rely on the path of my steps and my days

Suddenly my head says – these gray secret days

—

The rhythm must be solved, it is
pure survival

farewell
lines come and go
must be so
step by step   that is salvation

so so
and so on

leise leise
there is nothing else

in the meantime words fall
like rain, unexpectedly

order comes from the very
joy of struggle

The bliss of continuing
The sensation of striving

let the complaint wane
let pure plain kindness prevail

live attentively. *To follow the moments* (Thorild)

in the adoration of a single line
the disdain for aphorism

You Tend a Field

You tend a field
We keep a horse there

The field is lean. The horse's wither is wide

You hear about it on a Monday

Perhaps we should have chosen a mule

You are a smallholder
a piece of mother's land
it yielded wine, red milk
once upon a time

the land is there: and the wither, the horse
but no fly sheet. The urge to cover

Everything is incremental
you own a field, there will be a fly sheet
soon but no house as far as the eye reaches, it
is a meager freedom

Lamentations

Reading about the oak
that children set aflame
the six-hundred-year-old tree
fell across the road
looking at the stump, thinking of the trunk
that one could seek refuge in its crevice during the rain
  hoo hoo mor
step out again when the light returned
stand in the sun, in a cloud of detrius
knew all too well
that one day she would sink under the earth and
therefore become both overcast and light

Watching Pina dance
How she too has now departed gone vanished
Pina – that name reminds me
of a river, a namesake to the east

the soot
the muted face the veils
the nakedness of her arms

pulled through a landscape of scrap
hailed from a grimy neighborhood
near the highways, Ruhr

when she dances she moves in such a way
her face at once here and already gone
filthy like phlox
meanderingly white
a river she is

Thinking of Jonah
and all dwellers of the deep
their mouths filled with mud and seagrass, ensnared
entangled in their web

those who were pulled down or
let themselves sink

like when a whale turns
and goes down to the darkest deep
in the Barents Sea

the pressure a relief
to follow it, be drawn
out of your own internal depths drowning you

you my friend, were one of those
who wanted to sink so deep that it glowed when breath
burst the night into light

To listen to the psalter water
then you are present
in the tangled strands
fingers straining to form sound
and the tongue syllable after syllable: a do nai
that is all
to pronounce with patience
the name
you noble stern
dark demanding
being

Suddenly remember that I was reading when
they were carrying out your things
it was Nox frater nox, of course
it was. There goes the desk
it scratched against the stairs' throat
scraped off some plaster, a bald spot
emerged. Like when one has to carry out a body that died in its
bed, the impression lingering in the sheets. Now a chair, the scraping
sound sticks around, legs against stone. On his head he carries the black
stool you rested your feet on. Where are you now? I pulled out the brown
accordian-folded book. Anne Carson writes about her brother
in Nox, *I prowl him* – To prowl is to lurk around as if
roaming through the margins the lands and the air as if on the hunt for
the feeling of your attention

The departed
I think of you
that a consciousness could be
absent –
it cannot be the case. I believe that it lasts, remains
resurfaced like a waterlogged log
it lifted itself up off the floor in the middle of the room
it did not glow, no
it shined

Give the grieving a survival guide
a cure for melancholy
a daily allowance
two hours of work with a pencil
then
rest, music
steps and walks, rest
and translation
to transfer lines from one language to another
nibble on hard bread in the meantime
empty sips of water
prose step by step or dancing verses
watch them come forward
like in Ovid's Black Sea songs
feel the longing at work and strive to
see a line *unfold* beneath the hand

Words Around Mom

A blackbird sang and fluttered by, too close for comfort
it was black
so it wasn't her then
not this time

She comes and goes now that she's no longer here
now that she's passed   so it seems
a beam tones out, a trail fading into the mist

a moth when the clock rings eleven

a hand on my brow
a smile around the corner

To go out into the world without a mother in it
was an occasion
to caress the air

cower in the gravel

To rest in mother's arms
take in the scent of skin and wool

Mom said: Don't sulk
Mom said: Don't get stuck
Mom said nothing, just be. And pointed at the road

Mom, mystery from the forest
gentle goshawk

Without mom
now no one
in all the world

that the one corner of a square – is gone
or the tips of a triangle, one of them broken
the space inside – emptied out

I caress the air. Her presence
fills the entire space
And of course out there too

In every rosebush a mother
or somewhere else
along the gravel path
Smiling sweetly, sorrowfully

The Waters of Ovid

I have waded in the waters of Ovid
comfort for heavy thoughts one winter, transferring words from one
 language
to another, from several languages and interpretations
for I do not know Latin

the most alluring version of the *Lamentations* are by Darrieussecq
Marie, such courage to peel pure a text two thousand years old
from everything learned – sorry – ostentatious
to carve out the core of longing and sorrow

so that the words now sound

unscathed

took a few pages each day
ventured with them, struggled with the words
swept away by them

a pensum, like in the middle ages
yes, the daily allowance against melancholy
being exerted – work

to work means to exert yourself

is that all that remains
it is – almost everything

I translated the songs from the trip to the Black Sea

they disappeared into the deep night of the hard drive
were just wiped away –

back to the point: I don't know Latin, the origin
the words from *Les Tristes* reproduced here from memory
they surface like planks in the sea after a shipwreck

day and night
they are here

the lines are
literal planks
rugged, they take off with such speed

to hold tight to them
to hook word after word is to carry on, when this winter is over
much is over, much is left

what is left is half the kingdom
and the rest is
to be left behind

Thinking of Mehmed, my friend who gave me the first edition
"Tristia," far away from the pomegranate blossom, from *dengbêjen*
which comes from words that mean *voice* and
the one who gives the voice form, who sings
far away from his mother's words and all the while with them in his head
this friendliness in those brown eyes

the lines were highlighted with red strokes like traces of blood
the way of life, the way of flight, sanctuary, wounds
"take the book, read it my friend, be not afraid to lose it"
It is, after all, loss spoken outright

I have lost
nearly everything, and am still here
with my body

"little book go to the city I cannot enter"

the lines are planks
and air to breathe
space to look up

the text begins with an imperative – the flash of life –
speech to a book, a prayer to follow it to a place that no
longer can be seen
over waves and seas

that the book shall travel to the places that cannot be seen

to Rome, to the sun, to you
but away
to a place without retreat

the passage, reading it over and over again
imagining how it was when he swayed
across the sea in fear, Ovid in the waves, in the dark expanse
to know that it's happening in this moment

salt water splashed on my face
to open my mouth and the sea crashes in
to sink
it is here

to be stranded somewhere
to hear harsh voices, understand not a word

to see just one: to be entirely without
anything

wanting to grasp, hold onto something, the listing of a ship, like hands
caressing a book cover – a screen, no that's not right
a cover
in red or black
tangible like a wall

"I would like to be my book"

what I love the very most is the thought of that book
traveling in my stead, that it can become me
such faith in a book

and the image of the library, where it sneaks in among its
siblings, between their spines and goes into hiding
forbidden as it is

an undesirable, that can no longer exist, yes like the fate of a book
perhaps – an elder in exile, out of time and the world
who says with an unbroken voice: one knows not what becomes of
  their fate
where one shall be transported

o you
even said *swept away*

cry, go, poor book, journey to the place that I cannot enter
waiting for what will happen

write beneath time – so it says

how I would like to be my book
to be able to rest in your hands
when you hold me, look out with your gaze whether bright or stern

judge me not, but speak your mind
of the lines that go
go and go on

the elegy that pronounces the mania of writing
how he returns like a gladiator to the arena
like the enchained prisoners instinctively singing rhythmically
to endure

conjuring it, cursing poetry
and exalting it
"if I write then I don't sink"

a line resurfaces in the field of vision, it speaks of
Tomi and the Greek word for "cut"
that it was here Medea sliced her brother, scattered his body parts

they were collected, the head set on the skerry
the cliff where Ovid disembarked in his exile
away from all, without return
in Tomi

which sounds so soft
like a nose a cry a caress a child
the place where she took life for the first time

the region of barbarians where the flesh of song is flayed by
animalistic sounds or sharpened by crags
"I ought to hate poetry"

the description of a terrifying winter
of being truly frozen white, fish fastening in ice
and the fear of what can come over it, of invasion

to be entirely misunderstood
"I have forgotten my language
and have nothing to ask"

here he nakedly received his language
to say "the heart and the soul is all we have"

be in this water
sway among the waves
feel the splinters from the boat's wood in your sole, saltwater over
your face

the power of the enunciated

to cry out the fear of not knowing where we are headed
to feel that someone else has it much worse, an awful
thought, is a comfort

the lamentation that purifies

"I write to you"

my muses

"I will echo until the end of worlds
beyond the depths of the sea"

waves, two thousand years, perpetually here

go now and lay your hands upon this
book

Formulae of the Word

I collect lines, I collect sticks, I collect leaves and words
I divide devote and despair

In the word language there is age and gauge
It is palpable. E x p e r i e n c e would be the word
Something monotone and observant

To derive
etymology is no philosophy, but it amuses, leads us on – is fun

The impulse like the paths of ants

To write is not to play but not far way, perhaps a playful thought –
writing. That is to say
dance. To turn in place, to turn around, stand on your head
with your brow to the ground

Stand in the word-dwelling. *Abound on earth*

Dig around amongst the words
Drive the wild into the light! Pull up
and nurse the consonant root

Dikt, as if the word is sprained mid-way. Broken mid-line
It shouldn't sound like that. Bring forth and
bring along

Linje, longing to leap along with it. To just be drawn along
Resistance too. Articulated, tenacious language
Latin –

O how I would love to know Latin. The most physical of languages
The most tangible. Staves, levers, clockwork. A box of tools

Teach me to use fewer words. Teach me to use the plow
teach me to make use of
the harrow of which I speak

– It is a pin harrow, to be precise.
– Good, we like to be precise. (words from an unknown film)

Incantation . . .

Listen up now

In this resonance
my self ceases

in light spirals

sun-thirst frost-sieve

down falls the rain
up stands

the light of life
the darkness of living

Song, Turn

There is a season we sang
To everything
turn, turn, turn
there is a season
it rang so true
we danced

rocking like an ark, a great seabird
fluttering falling
casting itself up, and onward, again
heavy and happy

it was
The Byrds
it was then, and we didn't think it was the Preacher's words
once more resounding
about how everything has its time, now we know

and I almost forgot these unbridled steps but
some things still touch my heart
like the words and the notes Turn!
Turn! Turn!

in this era of sown hesitation
disappearing time
evaporating life
fall into dance
                    say it out loud, turn
the thought precedes – what happens

and then there was Dylan's diction
that permeated it all
that is the half of it, or nearly all
intonation
a voice's wax and wane
how it cuts through
from another realm, and here
excavated tunnels and rooms, far down and up
up among the clouds
blowing in the wind

at the world's end

so bore away, voice, you can go
through mountains
you are a wave without end

the song is a revenant

a pair of siblings from Solbacken, high over Helgasjön
spread your wings wide

as I wrote, a crowd of birds came and took everything in a swarm
every pale bilberry, in a stealth invasion, and was gone
no worries, it'll
grow back
at some point, like the song always does

Starling with blueberries in its mouth

Muffled Song

The silence that grows
after death
after a snowfall
I have wandered in
someone hums tones during the Passacaglia
in the heavy church air
blackened gold
closed eyes
brushed knees
two small globes, they have stopped
they have started
they have stopped and they start again
all has stopped
and it starts again
it has stopped
and all starts again

No, look it's snowing
I wake every morning with a song
in my mouth
since she's been gone
we tread on –
in the sun of summer –
yet is it still winter
And so we turn the page
Everything rises upwards
and disappears
a fire burns
it burns so lucidly
the body is a playground
the old bed
when the body burns or
sinks a pillar of song rises
everything becomes white white white

Voicegrass
which word the night bore
pulled you out of bed

voicegrass
a feeling strong as meadow
hold up the burgeoning thought

grass under the foot
straw like lines

the sounds of farewell, the words from her bed
thank you for the song

a lull, a hum, a song without words

Marsyas, Inscribed

Skin-sound and foliage
from a flowing body

towards the earth the brown
land's striated ground

so completely grounded, spirit
dangling   vulnerable vision out in the other

glade of silence
luminous leftover

your sheen – my wish
that the pencil should break and you flow
out

the tone
when it emerges from the carcass
a drop
falls
my skin slips away

a language of flesh
all I wished for

and the sound closes

what wound

what pain
inhabits this glade

to just look out   wait, to know it will be
altered

to let it happen

become
that bareness
the gestures without adhesive, without
syntax

a speech without words yanked out, thrown to the world   *the others*

a semblance   yes
nothing more

and gone   dissipated

to cross over

your blood became a flood   I dream of this
think *it's happening*

to wander
to wash
over
to dawn

what more is there

a sole tone-body

broken down and re-fused

again and again, to resonate

disperse, flow, diverge

disappear   transform

"Two dear things in the world: song and formula."

—MARINA TSVETAEVA

A FEEL FOR WHAT LANGUAGE CAN BE

Carin Franzén

In a neoliberal era characterized by ever increasing possibilities for more and more people to shape their lives as they wish, it may seem backwards to, as the great Swedish poet Gunnar Ekelöf did, profess "the art of the impossible." Yet in modernist aesthetics and its descendants, this attitude often emerges as a prerequisite for critical practice. The German artist Anselm Kiefer's 2005 diagnosis of contemporary aesthetics in the French newspaper *Le Monde* points in this direction:

> The earlier subversive formulation "art is life" has been distorted into pure mimicry. The war in the mind – the long road that the initial idea, the concept must take to get to its result has been reduced to a single point. Everything is possible, even though art is actually constituted by the fact that almost nothing is possible.

In Katarina Frostenson's condensed and fragmented art of writing, I see a remarkable control over this impossible art that seems to also resonate between Ekelöf and Kiefer.

In this collection, *The Space of Time* (published in Sweden as *Sånger och formler* in 2015), there is no direct reference to Kiefer, though his teacher Joseph Beuys' famous 1977 installation "Tallow" appears in lines such as "wrapped in brown / in Beuys' wax and feel / a longstanding yearning / to pursue." Across the collection's three sections—"Adrift," "In the Open," "Pain's Pathways"—one can parse out a double movement between linguistic impulse and sensory envelopment, a movement that on another level also juxtaposes language's material tangibility with a particular dispersion of words' potential meanings.

This double movement between collecting and scattering creates a peculiar rhythm, exemplified by the following lines in the first poem, "Januaria":

> to dissipate
> gentle dispersion and light sifting out through gaps
> in the clouds
> [...]
> and all the while language moves, whipped by the wind, torn
> into tissue
> [...]
> you will still be called song
> you who pull the barge, be diligent, language you are on
> guard
> someone must tighten the sail and embrace –
> [...]
> a first feeling of a future emerging of those words that endure
> and evade understanding but resound that seventh of January
> long
> forward in time

If we understand this double movement as an allusion to the multifaceted god Janus—he who opens and closes the gates of heavenly light and with his two faces can simultaneously see into the future and back into the past—we can then read "Januaria" as an associatively rich maxim not just for this collection of poems but also as the foundational rhythm of Frostenson's entire oeuvre. This double movement—the opening and the closing, the scattering and the collecting, but also the calling-forth of that which is lost to time but which also "resound[s] . . . forward in time"—punctuates Frostenson's linguistic inimitability. It also resembles a modernist aesthetic that unites a strong credence to artistic means of expression, to the transformative power of language, with an exploration of the borders and limitations of poetic language.

Sånger och formler was awarded the 2016 Nordic Council Literature Prize, with the committee describing the collection as "a story of life's physical and spiritual revelations, about the little things and the big things, and about humanity in the world." The motivation also accurately states that Frostenson's poems are "so apparently tight, yet actually very spacious" and open for transformation. The movement of language and the dispersion of meaning, as well as the poetic potential to represent life in its complexity, are singled out here as an initial driving force in Frostenson's writing, which for that very reason both repeats and perpetuates, reiterates and renews language with a ceaseless sensitivity that responds to the metamorphoses that take place in the world and in poetry.

It is this description of Frostenson's poetry that I want to take as a starting point to trace several features and paths which emerge from Frostenson's double movement and which have become increasingly perceptible in her poetry in recent decades. As many readers have noticed, her more recent work features both a more political tone turned towards the world, as well as an intimate voice that, among other things, retraces the footsteps of childhood.

And all the while language moves

This double movement in Frostenson's writing grows out of a poetic posture that can already be discerned in her debut *I mellan* (In between; 1978), but which eventually develops into an ever-clearer strategy of resistance against a contemporary social order—namely, global capitalism and neoliberal hegemony—that shapes the subject in the absolute name of self-interest. In *Sånger och formler,* it is as if Frostenson allows this domineering subject to speak out at the same time as she undermines its position:

> I set the limit for what I give each day
> what others, and which of them, are worth
> to not belong and still stay put is existence –

The speaker here appears to be a privileged Westerner standing before a new social reality where "the others," those forced into exile by poverty and war, can no longer be ignored—an economically minded subject who not only lets their self-interest determine where a given limit lies, but also what the other is worth and to what extent they belong. What is nevertheless insistent in this poem ("A Neighborhood") is the ability of language to shift the boundaries of subjectivity and thought, to transcend the established conditions of belonging and identity. It is the unfolding movement of the poem's associations that unsettles the domain of self-interest. The poem moves from the terror of our time and the politics of fear it stokes—"anything can be prey without warning, the laws are changed by . . . fear"—to the reality of homelessness that in turn invokes the memory of home, the longing for homecoming: "can you sense the scent of wisdom wafting from her, it was then and / it is here // that is home, among camps of strangers." This is how the poem shifts perspective from the self to the other. It is a critical practice founded in poetry's potential to be a counterlanguage (*motspråk*).

Thanks to her sensitive ear for the languages that surround and shape the human as a social being, Frostenson coaxes the poetic word to explore what lies beyond the *art of the possible* (*Kunst des Möglichen*), the pragmatic and realistic political mindset oriented around action and decision. This approach can be traced throughout modernism, and it was probably the Russian formalist Viktor Shklovsky who coined its most charged concept—defamiliarization (*ostranenie*)—in the essay "Art as Device" (1917): a linguistic alienation without which the automaticity of language that occurs within social community would consume life itself. Frostenson's continuation of this tradition does not just seek to counteract the automation and instrumentalization of language. Indeed, in this collection it is the value of literature itself that is at play: "the language of poetry may be dying." And one way to counteract its death can be as simple as returning to the already-written:

> Linger in a space with Marina Tsvetaeva and Birger Sjöberg
> Feel the current of language
> The crosspollination, the meeting of the unfamiliar
> So that you again get a feel for what language can be

With Frostenson (as with many other poets and artists who debuted towards the end of the twentieth century), the poetic strategy that provokes language to reveal its ability to unsettle and transform develops into a critique of the age of mass media. Through its "songs and formulae," the poem asserts itself as a countermovement against sanitized language, a notion Frostenson neatly sketches out in the early essay "Språket och den andra" (Language and the other; 1989) with her description of a language that has been entirely evacuated of wonder in our contemporary information-saturated society,

> a language that beams out that the world is here, entirely here, that it is entirely possible to manage, that, practically speaking, everything can be put in order. It is a language that is illuminated by its absence of the Other, the vague, the ambiguous, the dark. A blank language. A language without shadow.

If one follows Frostenson's poetry from her debut to this collection, one finds less a poetic universe and more a consistent poetic counterlanguage—one that is everything but turned away from the world. Frostenson opens up the poem towards a world concealed by a language consumed by mass media, instrumentalization and sensation, a world where everything can be extracted, that leaves nothing left to be said. In opposition to this logic, poetry maintains a different temporality. In one of the strongest poems in the collection, "The Waters of Ovid," reading, writing, and translating are brought into political reality in a way that unites a historical refugee scenario—the exile that Ovid recounts in *Tristia* and *Letters from the Black Sea*—with an ongoing reality:

> the passage, reading it over and over again
> imagining how it was when he swayed
> across the sea in fear, Ovid in the waves, in the dark expanse
> to know that it's happening in this moment

This is political poetry on several levels. Not only is the war and devastation of the present day a root note for the entire collection, but it also appears explicitly, such as in the poem "Silent Directive": "a single name can expose everything   you see the devastation in just / the names // Syria / Kobanî." The procedure of letting the geographical names convey their political, tragic reality is also found in the opening poem "Päronblom" (Pear blossom) of *Korallen* (The coral; 1999). Here the speaker finds themselves in a flowering valley emerging from a sleep violently interrupted by a cold reality:

> that slumber
> is not long
> it resembles the crash

a plummet into the valley where language is unknown
gravel, snow, grozny

When the Czech city of Grozny is articulated in the poem, a turn happens. The sensory description of the dale with its "burst pears, bees / the intoxication of sweet taste," and with a living history, transforms in the next line into a metonymic description of the ravages of war: "a leather shoe on frozen ground / the lips of this cold mouth." The turn from the introductory openness to existence in all its sensation and depth to a war-torn reality establishes a simultaneity that gives the poem a tragic deep structure and gestures beyond the individual events of war. If this political dimension has always existed in Frostenson's poetry in this twofold way, expressed via a uniquely poetic counterlanguage that responds to reality, then the very possibility of poetic writing is likewise at stake in *Sånger och formler*.

In her recent collections, Frostenson enters into what is known as the "Anthropocene," the age fatefully marked by humanity's impact on the earth's ecosystem, the environment, and the climate as a result of increased technological development and the commercial exploitation of natural resources. Facing a world inundated with growing environmental degradation ("all this plastic you have on your conscience"), with war and horror ("Syria, infusing, is the night"), one poem asks: "How should I / say / speak / think"? It asks the question at the same time as it formulates an answer. This is yet another feature of Frostenson's poetics: the uncertainty about the very meaning of poetry is written into poetic method itself. Frostenson has always set the boundaries and limitations of the poem against what one might call the high demands of modernism. But they nevertheless take on a more tangible significance in a time when the symbolic activity itself can be said to be in crisis, partly due to the kind of reality hunger that led Kiefer to speak of the pure "mimicry" of contemporary aesthetics, and partly due to the increasingly acute sociopolitical problems of our world, which in various ways call into question the very existence of art and literature.

Perhaps this is why the myth of Marsyas, the faun who challenged Apollo and was flayed alive as punishment, plays such a prominent role in Frostenson's later work. She adapts Ovid's story from the sixth book of the *Metamorphoses*, which despite its brevity nevertheless provides a detailed description of the cruel punishment and the skinless body, later poignantly portrayed by the Italian Renaissance artist Titian. In both *Karkas* (Carcass; 2004) and *Tre vägar* (Three paths; 2013), as well as in this collection, Frostenson recounts Ovid's story and the Renaissance painting in such an intense and vivid way that Marsyas emerges as a touchstone for Frostenson's poetics. Perhaps she points to Apollo, the god of art, to underline the skinless body of the faun as a formula for her own writing, as a credo for a poet who seeks to bring poetry's lofty claim back down to earth, as a way to make poetry open up to the corporeal vulnerability of life. As stated in the collection's final poem "Marsyas, Inscribed": "a language of flesh / all I wished for [. . .] a speech without words yanked out, thrown to the world *the others* [. . .]."

These are the words of a poetics turned towards the world, but if there is a reality hunger here, it does not lead to a metaphysics of presence or a dream of grasping reality directly. Frostenson continues to explore the possibilities and limitations of poetry with and through language, and in this sense the poet is faithful to the impossible art that both Ekelöf and Kiefer highlight as part of the modernist tradition. She can thus simultaneously state that art is "a semblance yes / nothing more" while emphasizing that this semblance is a way to reflect on the world and the fact that humanity has been given language to do so. Language is the way to a poetic world that can respond to the world as such. In Frostenson's poetry, we can see how that response always takes place through a double movement which simultaneously emphasizes the "semblance" of poetry alongside the everchanging force that appears in the final lines of "Marsyas, Inscribed": "disperse, flow, diverge / disappear transform".

The linguistic uniqueness and the distance from the noise of the world that was coded as negativity in modernism is thus revised into an affirmation. Poetic activity has a limit for Frostenson, but for that very reason it also has its own unique power that vibrates in a poetic echo chamber where motifs and themes from her own poems or from other writers, artists, and poets reappear and disperse across names and intertexts. Interestingly, this recycling corresponds to what we might today talk about in terms of ecology—an interplay between language and world that in poetry takes place on several levels—but which also reflects a contemporary preoccupation with ecological perspectives.

As formulated in *Sånger och formler*, it is a poetic practice that "rejoices in recycling" by returning to one's own surroundings, by entering into dialogue with the works of others. The collection's original title, basic theme and structure, for example, is 'recycled' from a beautiful quote by the Russian poet Marina Tsvetaeva (1892-1941) and placed as an epilogue: "Two dear things in the world: song and formula." The Russian poet's name, work and turbulent life during the Russian Revolution and Civil War, which drove her into exile and eventually led to her suicide, are interwoven into several poems as a kind of affectionate inner dialogue:

> Marina October apple astrakhan
> [. . .]
> you are virtually the only thing in my thoughts these days
> your existence – o how it morphed, the sound of rails, of
>   hooves, exuberance
> those silent rooms, the noose

Frostenson has likewise described Tsvetaeva's poetry as "extremely equilibristic in terms of sound," and the kind of modernist, artful, esoteric poem she represents could be seen as a counterpoint to Frostenson's own. The Russian poet nonetheless gives the collection its name, and in another poem Frostenson addresses her friend and colleague Birgitta Trotzig, for whom Tsvetaeva was an obvious elective affinity:

> I come across the Marina biography on my way into town
> the eye-deafening image of her on the cover
> I had forgotten that you wrote the foreword, Birgitta

The theme of mourning is woven throughout several of the collection's poems, be it of deceased friends, other poets and artists, as well as the unknown. Several poems in particular tread into, explore, and sing of the sorrow of losing one's own mother. But familiar aspects of Frostenson's poetic method also emerge, namely geographical locations as well as the speaker's own constantly evolving identity. For instance, the memory of the suburb where she grew up: "Hägersten is a kangaroo pouch in thought"; and the exploration of the boundaries of her own identity through the very name Frostenson: "in this resonance / my self ceases."

Sånger och formler is thus both innovative and reutilized. And in order to convey both the uniqueness and the echoes that resound in lines such as "By force must the song be written – / Sing anyway // All that sings, sings for the second time," I will now try to summarize a central poetic theme that emerges across Frostenson's almost five decades of writing.

All that sings, sings for the second time

Frostenson's poetry emphasizes the necessity of distance for the life of language and for the sense of life in the face of a contemporary tendency to abolish the boundary between world and language, between poem and life admidst an ever-present flow of information, opinions, and capital. This is an inclination that can be discerned in her writing of the 1980s and 1990s, but it finds a more specific articulation in the collections that have emerged since the millennium. At a time when the intimate space is well on its way to dissolving into the public, she writes in *Karkas* about a cityscape of:

> [. . .] a lone speaker who loudly
> expresses himself, speaks out into the air where
> they stand at the crosswalk, the red lights that have halted –
> the ticking – the shrill ringtones – the in-
> audibility yes as if perforated, pierced every ounce of
> silence shattered and stupefied

In the present collection, another consequence of Western technological development—waste—emerges, which in the poem "Trash Trail" intertwines with Frostenson's own poetic method, as it "rejoices in recycling":

> [. . .] all the waste you produce
> impossible to grasp, with neither hand nor mind, it is
>
> an unfathomable amount
>
> an ancient cell phone at the bottom of the bag
> I don't want to see
> your sad shell, o you've put in your time, poor thing
>
> amongst carrot peels and plastic, cheese sauce
> and envelopes and meeting notes, batteries

Rather than the intrusive "obscenity" of publicness that has previously preoccupied Frostenson's poetry, this collection is characterized by the global capitalism that has given rise to an absurd distribution of excess, waste, and poverty. Frostenson is a poet of her time. The political tone has in some ways become more explicit, but so has the biographical and metapoetic dimension that has always been present in her writing. Perhaps one could say that *Sånger och formler* is both more desperate and more settled than the works that preceded it. Nothing particularly new emerges here, but instead there is a honing of earlier themes which paradoxically also leads into a kind of disarming gesture, in turn making several poems unusually playful amongst the sorrow and seriousness: "To write is not to play but not far away, perhaps a playful thought – / writing." Frostenson has always confronted reality with wordplay—the sensitivity to words' fractured surfaces and transformations. It is a resistance, a poetic strategy that keeps "vague worlds alive in an / all too unblemished time," to quote a few lines from *Samtalet* (The conversation; 1987).

Frostenson's poetry is constantly on the lookout for opportunities to open up—indeed break open—language to the possibilities of transformation. This gives her poetry a distinctly dialogical, polyphonic character that includes the interpolation of elective affinities and an exploration of the materiality of language: "I collect lines, I collect sticks, I collect leaves and words / I divide devote and despair" as it goes in *Sånger och formler*. Poetic writing chisels out ambiguities, subjecting words to dispersal, displacement, and the creation of new meaning. It is a project that grows out of a modernist tradition. But Frostenson's poetry drills down into language and highlights the violence that can be present in naming and meaning, as well as in love, in the relationships with the world and with other people. In her poetry from the 1990s, this violence often appears in an interplay between subject and object, the seer and the seen, as in the collection *Joner* (Ions; 1991), which in many respects can be read as an exploration of the drama of gender difference. The later collections since the turn of the millennium onwards offer clearer expression of power imbalances between those who are well off and those who are oppressed—the refugee, the migrant, the beggar. As in the following lines from the poem "Orden mot" (Words towards) in *Flodtid* (Flood-hour; 2011):

When you hear the rattle of the dead language, you look up a
pair of eyes
there are no paperless, there are human faces
there were no refugees, there are bodies

Interpersonal violence can also be observed in the very representational force of writing, which is highlighted as an ethical dilemma in this collection:

the chasm

to sing of others
to sing can be to take over

Frostenson's own poetic method of countering the violence of representation—"to sing of others"—has always been about pursuing the ambiguity of language rather than espousing any moral conviction. The emphasis on the sensory side of language that social practice necessarily reduces is made audible and perceptible again. What is usually termed the poetic function of language is animated by body, drives, and passions. In this collection, the formula goes:

Dig around amongst the words
Drive the wild into the light! Pull up
and nurse the consonant-root

In this way, the recognizable and worn-out can be explored anew, opened up to the "other, the vague, the ambiguous, the dark," as Frostenson spoke of in the 1980s. Her poetic language has always sought to keep indeterminacy alive, to prevent it from being floodlit and perforated. But it does not, lest one suggest, lead to a return to mysticism. For Frostenson, the art of the impossible is a matter of fact. It is about accepting certain basic conditions of human existence, as is evident from the strong motto for *Sånger och formler*—kind of counter-psalm that nevertheless encompasses a hymnic longing for grace:

Words flow forth
The sun arrives
No shepherd tends
Everything exists

The unsentimental tone in Frostenson's poems suggests that neither melancholy nor nostalgia are guiding principles. It is significant that this tone resonates most clearly when it is childhood—the locus of nostalgia *par excellence*—that forms the focus in the poems which over the years could be dubbed "Hägersten-poems." Yet the biographical traces in Frostenson's poetry never become personal confessions; they are written with a will to evoke that which cannot be separated from a displacement of subjective experience in and through linguistic creation. This movement is liberating but also testifies to the fact that not everything can be said. A shadow remains. It is the dynamic of the pull backwards, to memories or other already-written texts, and forwards, through associations and linguistic play, that turns the transformation of the personal into a literary experience, i.e. into another place that always carries on. An earlier example from *Samtalet* is illustrative:

Everything within me shifts
and looks off   Away
the names, the words
the places: a heron on a stone
the birthplace
I stand and freeze in my name, its purity

In this poem, with the slightly ostentatious title "jAg" (I), there is certainly a biographical play with names: Katarina, which etymologically means "the pure one," and the word *frost* in Frostenson—"I stand and freeze in my name, its purity"—as well as the allusion to her "birthplace" of the Stockholm suburb Hägersten. But there is nothing private about Frostenson's intimacy, and I think it is dangerous to read her poetry as autobiographical. Poetry is another life that comes into being through "dispersion," as it goes in this collection's opening poem "Januaria." It is as if the poetic method disseminates the biographical—names, places—and allows it to merge with the human: "gets [it] to move // homo nomadus." And in the last section of the collection, the poetic dissemination of meaning is specified in a completely disarming way: "To derive / etymology is no philosophy, but it amuses, leads us on – is fun."

The play of poetic language leads away from the information that biography could have provided in a more conventional confession or hermeneutic search for a more original or definitive meaning. The poem deconstructs its own cipher, mixes up the keys and goes on its own way. Frostenson's linguistic play forces that which has not yet been crystalized to remain active and disperses that which has been fixed.

It is a poetics nurtured by the diversity of language and the world, dispelling any nostalgic longing for unity and union, or other beliefs that promise a solution to the complexities and transformations of existence. Frostenson's poetry opens up to landscapes, places, time-spaces, and "words flow forth," assembling in new formulas and songs in a time when "the language of poetry may be dying"—thus showing how poetry can be written when almost nothing is possible.

NOTES

"Turn"

Bruegel – Pieter Bruegel the Elder (1520-1569), Dutch/Flemish Renaissance painter, known for landscape paintings such as "Hunters in the Snow" and "The Tower of Babel"

"Trash Trail"

Il pianto della scavatrice – a poem by Italian poet Pier Paolo Pasolini. The line above refers to his mysterious and unsolved murder

"Silent Directive"

Hägersten – "Heron Stone," southern urban district of Stockholm on Liljeholmen island, where Frostenson grew up

Marina Tsvetaeva – (1892–1941) one of the greatest symbolist Russian poets

Birger Sjöberg – (1885-1929) Swedish poet, novelist, and popular songwriter

Kobanî – Kurdish-majority city in northern Syria, immediately south of Turkish border, location of the Siege of Kobanî in September 2014

"An Evanescence"

Sergels Torg – a major public square in Stockholm, constructed in the 1960's

"Over Here"

Sveavägen – a major street in Stockholm, originating at Sergels Torg and continuing north in a straight line

"Mania/Lines"

Contrapunctus 14 – an unfinished part of Bach's *The Art of the Fugue*

"Song of the Brook"

Beuys' wax – Joseph Beuys (1921-1986) was a German artist, teacher and theorist, founder of the Fluxus movement

"Voicegrass"

Gullberg – Hjalmar Gullberg (1898-1961), Swedish poet and translator

"The Street's Name"

Elsa Brändström – a Russian-born Swedish nurse and philanthropist, known as the "Angel of Siberia" (*Engel von Sibirien*), serving as a nurse in World War I, and later fundraising for numerous aid organizations and caring for former POWs in Germany and founding children's homes until her death shortly after the end of World War II

"Siberian Song"

Katinka – feminine name, in diminutive form Katerina, meaning "pure"

Sakhalin – a Russian island in the Pacific north of the Japanese archipelago

"Marina"

Birgitta – Birgitta Trotzig (1929-2011), Swedish author

Slottsbacken – "Castle Street," street running through the Gamla stan (old town) in Stockholm, from the Stockholm cathedral and royal palace to the main public square

"Existence"

Anita Björk – (1923-2012) Swedish stage/film actress, at one time married to Swedish writer Stig Dagerman

Tintomara – an intersex character in C.J.L. Almquist's 1834 novel *The Queen's Jewels*, and the titular character of the film based on the novel. An enduringly popular character in Swedish literature

Lund – a university town in southern Sweden, also known for its cathedral

Dagerman's *Burnt Child* – a 1948 psychological realist novel by Stig Dagerman (1923-1954), written in France about the same time as his reportage *German Autumn*. Centers on teenager Bengt and his father; the mother has recently died and Bengt accuses his father of not respecting his dead mother, and attempts to hinder a new woman from taking her place while at the same time feeling a forbidden attraction to her

Tumba – A small town in Sweden

"Grain"

Rekola and Seiler – Mirkka Rekola (1931–2014), Finnish writer; Lutz Seiler, (b. 1963), German poet and novelist

Thorild – Thomas Thorild (1759-1808), Swedish poet, critic, feminist and philosopher

"Lamentations"

Pina – Pina Bausch (1940-2009), German dancer and choreographer

"Song, Turn"

Solbacken – a royal villa in the city of Växjö

Helgasjön – a lake in the Växjö municipality in south province of Småland, Sweden

ACKNOWLEDGMENTS

Some of the poems from this collection have been previously published, generally in slightly different versions, in the following venues:

"Silent Directive" and "Muffled Song" in *Tupelo Quarterly*

"The Brook – Song" and "Tomorrows" in *Anthropocene*

"Siberian Song" in *Oxonian Review*

"Voicegrass" and "Incantation . . . " in *Plume*

"The Waters of Ovid" in *Denver Quarterly*

"Heron Lands" in *The Dodge*

"The Street's Name" in *The Fourth River*

"Mania/Lines" in *The Hopkins Review*

Carin Franzén's essay originally appeared in Swedish in the 2017 issue of *Norsk litterær årbok*, which annually publishes an essay on the winner of the previous year's Nordic Council Literature Prize. It has been translated and slightly edited here.

KATARINA FROSTENSON is one of the most notable living Nordic poets. The author of over twenty books, her work has had a major influence on Swedish poetry since the 1980s. She has in addition written dramas, prose, and an opera libretto, and translated works by Duras, Bataille, Bove, and Michaux. Frostenson has received nearly every literary prize in Sweden and many across European. Her writing has been translated into over a dozen languages ranging from French, German, Italian, and Spanish to Belarusian, Croatian, Polish, and Serbian. In 2003, she was made a Chevalier of the French Legion of Honor in recognition of her services to literature and in 2016 was awarded the Nordic Council Literature Prize—Scandinavia's most prestigious literary honor—for the present collection, which has also been translated into French and Italian. In 2019-2021, she released the autofictional trilogy *K*, *F*, and *A*, the first of which also premiered as a stage play in October 2022 at the Folkteatern in Gothenburg. Her latest book, *Alma*, appeared in 2023.

BRADLEY HARMON is a writer, translator and scholar of Nordic and German literature, film, and philosophy. A Ph.D. candidate at Johns Hopkins University, he has been an American-Scandinavian Foundation fellow to Sweden, a Fulbright fellow to Germany, and an Emerging Translator Mentee with the American Literary Translator's Association. He also is co-editor of the volume *Rilke and the Horizons of Phenomenology* (De Gruyter, 2025) and a special dossier on translation and literary citizenship in the American academy (*MLN* 138.5, 2023). *The Space of Time* is his debut book of literary translation.

CARIN FRANZÉN is a professor of comparative literature at Stockholm University. Among her many books are *Translating Feeling: On Julia Kristeva's Psychoanalytical Poetics* (1995), *In the Beginning was the Word: Essays on Literary Experience* (2002), *Towards a Literary Ethics: On Birgitta Trotzig and Katarina Frostenson* (2007), *The Art of the Impossible: Essays on Literature and Psychoanalysis* (2010), *My Love I Gave Him Not: Courtly Love as Feminine Strategy* (2012), *When We Speak of Ourselves* (2018) and *Free Thinking: Female Libertines and Another Humanism* (2023). Franzén has also translated into Swedish books by Alan Badiou, Michel Foucault, and Jacques Lacan, as well as edited several volumes and textbooks on literary theory and history. She received the Swedish Academy's Dobloug Prize in recognition of her distinguished career as a literature scholar in 2019.